D0255642

need to know?

Body language

The secret language of body gestures and postures
that reveal what we really think and mean

Carolyn Boyes

Collins

First published in 2005 by Collins
an imprint of
HarperCollins Publishers
77–85 Fulham Palace Road
London w6 8jb

www.collins.co.uk

A catalogue record for this book is available from
the British Library

Designed and produced by Airedale Publishing
Art Director: Ruth Prentice
Designer: Hannah Attwell
Editor: Helen Ridge
DTP/Colour: Max Newton
All Photography by David Murphy except:
page 17 Groucho Marx © Rex Features/Everett Collection
page 65 Prince Charles © Tim Graham/CORBIS SYGMA
page 85 Japanese man © Bruce Burkhardt/CORBIS
page 95 The Queen © Tim Graham/CORBIS
page 163 George Bush © Brooks Kraft/CORBIS

For HarperCollins
Series Design: Mark Thomson

Back cover photographs: David Murphy

ISBN 0 00 720594 5

Pre-press by F.E. Burman, London
Printed and bound by Printing Express Ltd,
Hong Kong

Contents

Introduction 6

1   **Basics of body language** 14

2   **Eyes, face and head** 30

3   **Hands, arms and legs** 46

4   **Body and touch** 58

5   **Territory and personal space** 70

6   **Meeting, greeting and saying goodbye** 86

7   **Getting on well** 100

8   **Attraction and dating** 112

9   **Negativity: boredom, discomfort and stress** 130

10   **Lying, deceit and insincerity** 144

11   **Power, dominance and submission** 158

12   **Getting on at work** 172

Need to know more? 190

Index 191

Introduction

What do the gestures you use mean? How can you interpret what a person is really thinking about when they are talking to you? How can you become a better communicator? Communication is a process in which two people influence each other through giving and receiving information. One of the channels we use to communicate information is speech, or verbal language. But without words, you can still communicate through the oldest human language – body language, also known as nonverbal communication.

What is body language?

Every time you are face to face with another human being you speak to them through your body. The body has many ways to communicate: lavish gestures like waving, movements such as changes in the way we stand or sit, or in the position and directions of the head and eyes, as well as facial expressions and even the tiniest twitch of a muscle.

Any way in which you behave that can be seen by the other person as having a meaning is a form of language. Whatever words you choose to use in a conversation, it is inevitable that you are also talking in body language at the same time.

People watching

Understanding body language can make an enormous difference to every part of your life. When you see a picture in a magazine of a group of people, do you find that as you are looking at them you are wondering what they really think about each other? Whether watching celebrities on TV, observing office politics or meeting friends socially, we all spend time looking at other people and trying to work out what their behaviour really means.

Why we trust and distrust people

There are people you like the moment you meet them. Before they even begin talking they seem friendly and trustworthy. But what about the opposite experience? You've probably also had the feeling that you didn't trust someone when you first began talking to them.

The fact that you like or dislike someone doesn't always seem to make sense. What's being said may sound fine in both cases, but your brain is telling you something about the other person. You've got a gut feeling. If you like them, it is because they are sending out all the 'right' signals. If something seems wrong, it is probably because their verbal and nonverbal messages are different. They may have made some tiny involuntary movement that is giving a different message from what they are saying. Probably neither of you realizes consciously what has happened, but you have picked up the discrepancy between what they are saying and doing.

What does body language do?

Body language is a window into what's going on inside your mind. Each and every movement reveals your true feelings about the other person or the situation. As you transmit these feelings, in return you receive and interpret messages about the other person's attitudes towards you through their body language.

Gestures and movements occur when you are speaking but they may also be used as a substitute for words. Their message may support the verbal message or undermine it. What is deliberately not said verbally is often said nonverbally.

Deliberate or involuntary?

Most body language is spontaneous and outside your conscious awareness. However some gestures are deliberate. If you want to become a charismatic communicator, you need to be as effective in your physical communication as you are in your words. Great communicators are very aware of their whole communication and learn to control the messages they transmit through their bodies.

History of body language

Our knowledge of nonverbal communication has grown enormously over the last 30 years or so. Anthropologists and researchers in psychology, sociology and language have all researched how body language works. Not all body language is an exact science, but there is now more agreement about the probable meanings of gestures and movements.

Early history

The first people to look at how speech and gestures were related to each other were the Ancient Greeks and Romans. Hippocrates and Aristotle both commented on how our personalities throw up differences between us. The Romans recognized that it wasn't just words that made a great orator. They laid down a whole range of gestures to accompany the delivery of speeches.

Two thousand years ago, Cicero, the Roman philosopher (c.106–43 BC), suggested that the body's actions expressed 'the sentiments and passions' of the soul. He saw that the body, words, expressions and gestures were used as a whole to make up an instrument of communication.

English history

The first academic work in English to look at gestures came in the 17th century. John Bulwer's *Chirologia: The Natural History of the Hand* (1644) looked at the meaning and use of over one hundred hand gestures. He went on to write *Pathomyotamia* (1649), having been inspired by Francis Bacon who wrote *The Advancement of Learning* (1605) and made a link between gestures and what the speaker was feeling as he spoke. Bacon saw nonverbal language as the most natural form of language because it was not dependent on the country you came from or the language you spoke. He believed that listening and looking were equally important in understanding conversation.

18th and 19th centuries

At the end of the 18th century, Abbé L'Epée (1712–89) in France began to teach sign language to the deaf, showing them how to use gestures rather than force them to make any kind of attempt to use words or sounds. The next English work on gesture, though, was Gilbert Austin's *Chironomia* in 1806. He focused on how gestures could be used to accompany words to make speech-making more effective. Through this work he influenced the teaching of elocution in schools.

Throughout the 19th century, interest grew among actors and teachers of pantomime as to how feelings could be shown using movements of the hands and face.

Charles Darwin

In the same century, the naturalist Charles Darwin published *The Expression of the Emotions in Man and Animals* (1872). He recognized the links between humans and apes, pointing out how both species expressed their emotions through facial expressions. He suggested that monkeys and humans use sounds as well as nonverbal communication for mating reasons: in order to call out and attract the opposite sex.

Darwin inspired the study of animal behaviour (ethology) and research across disciplines such as psychology, zoology and archaeology into communication. However, it took another century before key research into the origins of language began to emerge.

20th century

In 1921, *The Language of Gestures* by Wilhelm Wundt, a key figure in the history of experimental psychology, was published. He concluded that gestures were a mirror into the emotions and inner world of a speaker.

Recent history

However, it wasn't until the 1950s that research on a larger scale began. The anthropologist Gregory Bateson in the 1960s focused on the idea that words can portray abstract ideas and thoughts but body language has a different function: to show emotions that are crucial to how you form relationships. Like psychologists since, he emphasized that there could be conflicts between verbal and nonverbal expression. A speaker can contradict himself even as he speaks.

One of the most influential writers in recent decades has been the zoologist Desmond Morris. He published *The Naked Ape* in 1967 and linked body language to people's animal nature.

Specific studies continuing to look at the meaning of different gestures have most recently been published by psychologists such as Peter Collett and Geoffrey Beattie.

Study of body language

The study of body language has now evolved into several areas.

▶ **Kinesics:** This is the study of body movements – hand movements, head nods, shifts in gaze and facial expressions – and, especially, how they are used when you are speaking. It looks at how this body language is used to communicate and to display mental and emotional states.

  Kinesics was first developed by an American anthropologist from the Eastern Pennsylvania Psychiatric Research Institute, Ray L. Birdwhistell. He published *Introduction to Kinesics* in the 1950s, in which, by analysing people talking to each other, he examined how gestures were used to emphasize and illustrate conversation. He believed that the meaning of body language was dependent on the context in which it took place.

  Paul Ekman, a psychiatrist from the University of California, filmed interviews with psychiatric patients who were trying to get released from hospital. His studies confirmed the importance of nonverbal behaviour, or leakage, in spotting deception. In the 1970s, Albert Scheflen, a psychiatrist from the USA, showed how individuals habitually used certain sequences of actions and also mirrored other people with whom they felt comfortable.

▶ **Proxemics:** This is the study of personal territory and space: the distance between people when they are talking or doing things together. For example, sitting next to somebody communicates a different message from sitting opposite somebody.

The idea of personal space came in the 1960s from the ideas of Robert Sommer, an American psychologist, who realized that his patients preferred to keep certain distances between themselves and others.

The person who showed that cultural and biological rules determine how you use space and communicate emotions was Edward T. Hall, the American anthropologist and author of *The Silent Language* (1959). He set out the different zones people operate in according to the social context and their status.

In the 1980s, Vrugt and Kerkstra confirmed the differences between the sexes, saying that when strangers meet, women stand closer to the other person than men.

▶ **Haptics:** This is the study of touch. It looks at how touch takes place during conversations, and the effect of touching and being touched.

▶ **Paralanguage:** This refers to the nonverbal accompaniments of conversation: how the voice is used to accompany speech. A key figure in this area is Edward Sapir, who, in the 1920s, wrote about speech as an aspect of personality.

Why learn body language now?

Understanding others: Because of the huge growth in research over the last 40 years, it is clear how important body language is to how people relate to each other. It is also evident that the very tiniest movements can provide us with a window on the human mind.

It is human nature to be curious. We all want to know why someone acts as they do or why they say certain things. All human beings are different, and the differences can frustrate as well as arouse curiosity. You can learn to pick up nonverbal clues from others to predict what they are thinking and what they may do in a given situation.

Body language can let you know who to trust and who to be wary of. It gives you good reasons to carry on talking to another person or to cease communication.

Making yourself a better communicator: Each of us has a series of habits we use when we communicate. We are not compelled biologically to behave in certain ways but we do inevitably develop familiar and comfortable ways of being.

Through understanding body language, you can learn to change these habits to make your communication most effective in particular contexts and circumstances.

Through insights into the way that other people think and communicate, you can also learn to influence how they see you, and forge stronger relationships with them.

The key to good communication is flexibility. You can learn to speak in the language of whoever you come into contact with, so that they receive a message you want them to have, rather than one you communicate by accident.

What this book does

This book is intended to help you become a skilled reader and user of body language.

The first part of the book takes you through the basics of your body, summarizing the main movements and gestures we all use and allowing you to become acquainted with some differences in cultural expressions and behaviour.

Your ability to do this in each and every situation may make the difference between getting a date, passing an interview or winning a business deal. So, in later chapters, body language is applied to different contexts.

How can you spot a liar? How does your colleague show they're the boss? Is that person attracted to you? The answers to all these questions are given, as well as tips on cultural variations to make sure you can communicate effectively in different environments.

As you read this book, enjoy learning to read other people too. Most of all, enjoy revealing the secrets of your own body language!

1 Basics of body language

If you are not sure what someone really means, trust their body to tell you the truth, rather than their words. This chapter sets out the basics of body language, and looks at different types of body language, universal expressions of emotions and common gestures.

The Basics

The majority of people are very conscious of the words they use. You learn your native language from those around you, which is usually your family, and you refine your use of speech by learning the rules of grammar and the importance of good communication while you are at school.

However, few people, unless they have been on a presentation or communication training course, learn much about what their bodies are saying about them. But it is possible at any stage of your life to learn to use the wordless part of language. You can learn to use different gestures and body movements deliberately to be an effective communicator in different situations. You can also learn to read other people's body language to find out what secret thoughts and emotions lie behind their words.

must know

How we communicate

It is thought that around 93 per cent of our language comes from gestures, posture and facial expressions and the way in which we use our voices.

In the 1970s, Albert Mehrabian, a psychology professor, produced the model of communication used most now. He established that:

► around 7–10 per cent of the meaning we communicate comes through our actual words
► 38 per cent is the way in which the words are said: the tone, pitch and speed of the voice
► 55 per cent of the message comes from the body: gestures and facial expressions

The Mehrabian model cannot be applied precisely to any communication situation. Obviously, if you are speaking on the telephone, then your voice becomes a more effective medium for communication than the position of your hands. But even when you are having a telephone conversation, for example, how you stand or sit will influence your breathing and your voice, meaning that the role of the body as a communicator is still important.

The Mehrabian model acts as a useful guide and reminder that words alone can be, and are, frequently misunderstood.

Nature versus Nurture

Nature: Some gestures seem to be innate. We do not learn them but they have developed in us as part of our unconscious animal behaviour. The primary emotions such as fear and happiness are pretty much universal wherever we go. Likewise, blushing is a sign of embarrassment in all cultures. Shrugging and smiling are also universal gestures.

Nurture: Some gestures are learned as part of our social and cultural conditioning. They may be learned by us because of expectations about how a woman or a man should behave within a culture. These tend to be obvious to us. It is easy to notice when another person is behaving outside the norms of society's expectations. For example, how you are expected to eat a meal or sit vary in different cultures.

Other gestures are used automatically. You will have an unconscious reaction to the automatic gestures of another person and are unlikely to analyse their meaning.

Personal signatures
Some gestures are unique to an individual, who will use them habitually. These are known as signature gestures. Impersonators on TV pick up on these immediately so that the viewer knows at once who is being imitated.

▷ **Prince Charles** often fiddles with his shirt cufflinks before facing a crowd of people, betraying his nervousness. He also rubs his ear lobe when he is self-conscious.
▷ **Prince William** straightens his tie when he is about to walk in front of an audience. He marks a threshold between his private space and being in public.
▷ **Adolf Hitler** often adopted a fig-leaf pose, standing with his hands in front of his crotch.
▷ **Princess Diana** looked at people through her eyelashes with her head turned down.
▷ **Roger Moore** is known for raising a single eyebrow.
▷ **Groucho Marx** painted on eyebrows that he raised and lowered to make us laugh.

Groucho Marx's signature gesture was to raise and lower his eyebrows.

First impressions

In fact, first impressions of a person are formed in only around ten seconds. Our intuition about a new acquaintance is primarily influenced by how we feel about the way they are expressing themselves through their bodies. We do not necessarily know why we have reacted to them with like, dislike or trust, but it is because of how we are culturally and instinctively conditioned to interpret the communication they are sending us.

Watch for clusters of gestures to reveal emotion. Crossing the arms can have several meanings...

But when breaking eye contact is added, the person may be feeling negative.

Types of body language

In the 1970s, Paul Ekman, a researcher from the University of California, together with his colleague Wallace Friesen, were influential in showing how peoples' feelings can be worked out from careful examination of different facial expressions. They also divided body language into the following areas.

▶ Gestures made at the same time as you speak are called illustrators. They don't stand alone and substitute for words, but are used to describe or clarify the point that you are making.

▶ Affect displays are unconscious gestures. They encompass changes in facial expressions, movements of the arms and legs, how you stand and how much space you use. All of these give clues as to how you are feeling inside, and whether that is a positive or a negative feeling.

▶ Adaptors also relate to how you feel, and, they are also usually unconscious gestures. If you feel negative, you may try to handle the emotion by changing or adapting your body language. However, these are gestures that are focused towards the body. For example, if you are stressed, you might clench your fist, chew your hair or touch your face.

▶ Regulators are used to indicate that a conversation is continuing, whether or not the people are actually speaking. The use of regulators varies between cultures. Movements and gestures like nodding or simply looking at the other person are used to acknowledge participation.

▶ Different cultures and societies use different gestures deliberately to replace words. These are known as emblems, and may also be determined by other factors such as whether you are a man or a woman. Examples of emblems are the OK sign, the thumbs-up sign and obscene gestures.

Universal expressions

There are a few facial expressions that go across cultural boundaries. Smiles are universal, as are the facial expressions used to show emotions such as anger, happiness, surprise, disgust, fear and sadness.

An angry person tenses their lips and narrows their eyes.

The lower part of the face relaxes when you are happy. The teeth are visible and the eyes smile.

Anger

Angry people contract and lower their eyebrows to produce a frown. Wrinkles form over the bridge of the nose. The eyes are narrowed and staring. They may 'flash' with anger in movement. The lips are pressed tightly together and the jaw is tense and in a biting position. In some people the nostrils may flare. Babies can show anger from the time they are three months old.

This facial expression will be accompanied by other body movements such as the hands forming fists, jerking of the head and aggressive postures like placing the hands on the hips.

Happiness

When people are happy, they smile, laugh or even cry. Babies show signs of happiness when they are around five months old.

Happiness affects the lower face and the area around the eyes. The mouth turns out to the sides and upwards, often making the teeth visible. With genuine happiness, wrinkles, or crow's-feet, form around the eyes at the same time as an involuntary smile forms in the mouth. A genuine happy smile is symmetrical and causes the cheeks to bulge.

Surprise

With surprise, your eyes widen and open to expose the whites of the eyes. The eyebrows are raised and the forehead wrinkles. The mouth is loose and relaxed, and the bottom lip drops, as does the jaw.

Fear

Fear is a reaction to the body's fight or flight response.

Babies show signs of fear as young as five months.

Fear may lead to tears and a general trembling throughout the body. All the muscles of the body become tense and the skin may be pale. As you begin to feel fear, the palms of the hands are likely to be sweaty.

Fear shows in the face through increased blinking of the eyes, and also staring 'flashbulb' eyes, where the eyelids are pulled upwards to show the whites of the eyes and the eyeballs protrude. The pupils are dilated. The mouth is taut and pulled back. The lips tremble and may be accompanied by chattering teeth. There is sometimes throat clearing, and the breathing rate may increase as adrenalin is produced in the body.

The eyes open wide when you are surprised, and the jaw drops.

Fear shows in increased muscle tension in the face and body, and in staring eyes.

Sadness

Sadness is often accompanied by crying or tears welling up within the eyes. The face begins to droop and the muscles of the face become slack. The mouth turns down and the lips may tremble. The eyebrows rise slightly at the inner ends, producing wrinkles across the top of the nose.

Disgust

If you look at the mouth of someone who feels disgust, you will notice the upper lip is curled and pulled back, and the lower lip is lowered. The tongue moves forward and protrudes. The nose is drawn up and wrinkles form across the bridge. The nostrils are raised. The cheeks move up. The eyes narrow and partly close. The inner corners of the eyebrows are lowered to produce a frown. The lower eyelids are raised, producing wrinkles around the eyes.

Sadness shows in slack muscles in the face. The eyelids droop and the eyebrows frown, causing wrinkles across the top of the nose.

When we are disgusted, we narrow the eyes, as if we don't want to see whatever it is that has disgusted us.

Reading emotions

Facial expressions are not a foolproof guide to our emotions. When experimenters have shown pictures of people in different emotional states to a range of men and women, less than half of them have accurately guessed what the other person was feeling. Women are better than men at reading emotions. In some research, men show no better rate of identifying emotion than would happen by random chance.

Most people expect to read emotions on the face, but this is the area that can be controlled. Emotion does link with facial expression but we can also deliberately try to disguise what we are feeling by changing our expression. Our face can often lie more effectively than the rest of the body.

If you are trying to guess what someone else is feeling, look at the whole body. The lower half of the body is a particularly good signaller of emotions because we often forget to mask it. It takes longer for us to react in our limbs to a change of mood than it does in our face, but as most people do not try to control their legs and feet, they become a good place to start looking for clues.

Sometimes body changes are totally uncontrollable by us unless we are able to change our emotional state from the inside. The body may react to fear or anger or embarrassment by changing temperature or colour. Deep feelings show up in the form of blushing, sweating or blinking, and even in the shallowness and depth of breathing.

Once you become alert to the full range of deliberate and voluntary signals that people make, you will become very adept at picking up changes in body language.

Open and closed body language

Two of the basic clusters of gestures and movements that you will observe can be interpreted as open and closed body language – in other words, being relaxed and open to other people, or closed and defensive. When you change your body language, you show that there has been some change in your relationship with the other person: you are responding to something in the situation in a positive or negative way.

Closed body language

If you are threatened, you make your body smaller and put barriers in front of yourself as protection. A cluster of movements closes the body in by bringing the limbs close to the body and using contained gestures. This may signal either that you are showing you are not a threat or that you are uncomfortable with another person. Closed body language is also used when you want to hide your true thoughts, for example when you are lying. Some typical closed body movements you may observe in others are tense shoulders and arms, crossed arms and legs, arms and legs resting tensely on a table or chair or tucked behind the body with the eyes looking away from you or at the ground.

Open body language

When you open up your body to other people, it shows you are feeling positive about them or the situation you are in.

The main indicators of open body language are a lack of barriers. You open up your body to be

must know

Knowing yourself
▷ Body language is very effective for understanding ourselves.
▷ Watch your own reaction in conversations.
▷ Why are you adopting a closed stance? Who are you relaxed with? What is it about the other person that is making you look away?
▷ If you change your gestures, what happens to your attitude to the other person? If you open up, do you feel friendlier towards the other person? If you close down, do you feel less friendly?

Closed body language   **Open body language**

exposed and vulnerable to other people. Your arm and leg
gestures will therefore look either free and animated or slow
but generous. Your legs may be stretched out when sitting
or be in a parallel stance when standing. The feet may point
outwards. The palms of the hands may also be exposed.

   The message of such postures is 'I am relaxed so I can
expose myself to attack because I am powerful', or simply
'I am relaxed and comfortable'.

WATCH OUT

The ways in which introverts and extraverts react to conversations are very
different. Introverts find that too much interaction drains their energy,
whereas extroverts want stimulation. When they are talking together,
extroverts can easily overstimulate introverts, who then react by closing
their body language. Look out for the signs in introverts – an indication
that they need to have some space.

Universal and culturally specific gestures

Although some gestures are found the world over, others are specific to certain societies, cultures and countries. A gesture that is used to replace a word or phrase can have a neutral or positive meaning in one country yet be negative or rude in another.

Hand gestures

Many hand gestures are culturally specific. Here are a few that you will encounter around the world.

In most Western cultures, pressing the thumb and forefinger together to form a circle means OK. In Latin America and Germany, it is an insult, and in the Middle East an obscenity.

▶ **Beckoning:** In the UK, we beckon with the fingers and palm facing up. In Asia, beckoning gestures are made with the hand facing down.

▶ **Pointing:** In Western cultures, people are most likely to use a finger to point with, though the feet are often used as well. Be careful in Arab countries and some parts of Asia where pointing with your shoe is considered very rude.

▶ **Sticking the thumb out:** In the UK and USA, sticking a thumb out while standing at the side of the road means you want a lift. In Nigeria it is an insult, and it can be in Australia, too.

▶ **Crossing the fingers:** In the UK and USA, this is a wish for good luck.

▶ **Shaking the finger from side to side:** In the UK and USA, this is a sign of telling somebody off.

In the West, a V-sign made with the palm facing the other person means victory. When the palm is turned away, it is an insult. In Japan, both forms are used as positive gestures.

Tapping the nose in the West is an overt sign that you are feeling suspicious.

Circling a finger by the temple or tapping the forehead means 'that person is crazy'.

Shaking the fist means 'I am angry' and is a threat of aggression.

A thumbs-up sign in North America and the UK means 'it is good'.

Rubbing your hands together means 'I am cold' or 'I am excited about something'.

Putting the hands together and resting your head on them means 'I am sleepy'.

Universal gestures

Finally, as the world gets smaller, you might think that all countries would have adopted the same gestures to mean the same things. But some gestures do have different meanings between cultures.

- **Turning your back on someone:** This is rude in most cultures.
- **Shaking and nodding the head:** Shaking the head does not always mean 'no'. In Greece, Bulgaria, Turkey and Iran, it may mean 'yes', and nodding the head may mean 'no'.

Shoulder shrugging is found in all cultures, though the meaning is not always the same.

When someone winks at you, they are showing you affection or complicity.

Patting or rubbing the stomach in a circular movement means 'I am hungry'.

In the West, sticking out your tongue at another person is a deliberate insult.

Faking it

Here is a big warning sign before you go any further: faking body language is not easy.

You can only control your own body language so far. There are so many muscles in the human body that it is impossible to think about all of them. The face alone has 90 muscles. There will always be some leakage of your true feelings, even if you are very good at controlling your body.

This means that if you try to fake your body language in a purely mechanistic way, you will give out mixed messages and may seem untrustworthy or confused. If you uncross your arms and legs, it will not convince anyone you are open if you cannot look them in the eye at the same time.

We have all seen presenters and politicians on television who look shifty or uncomfortable. That is because they have been taught how to present themselves in a powerful way but they still have insecurities that leak out in their movements.

The best way to change your body language is to change how you are feeling inside. Changing your emotional state changes your behaviour automatically. Actors know this. They are believable because they work inside out. They feel the emotions they are acting by entering fully into another world.

You can do this, too. Faking body language is possible. You can look more powerful or learn to attract a partner more easily. But make sure you are very thorough in the way you go about it.

Final warning

It is important to be very aware of body language associated with different cultures. But bear in mind that even within a country or city there may be cultural differences between groups of individuals. Everybody is different and has different habits. The best way to understand body language is to learn what most people mean by single gestures or clusters of gestures, and, at the same time, get to know a person's habits within different contexts, so you can spot changes in gestures as a warning of a change in mood.

WANT TO KNOW MORE?

▷ Facial expressions
   See chapter 2
   Eyes, face and head
▷ Closed body language
   See chapter 9
   Negativity
▷ Open body language
   See chapter 7
   Getting on well

2 Eyes, face and head

If you want to see whether someone is happy or sad, first look at their face. Because our facial expressions are partly under our control, the face is the centre of our nonverbal communication. You can use a frown or smile to accent and underline your words. It is also a home to numerous unconscious micro-movements that give away your true thoughts and emotions. The focal point of the face and the body is the eyes – the most important means of body language you have.

The Eyes

According to Leonardo da Vinci, the eyes are the mirror to the soul. Their great power as a means of communication is shown in the number of expressions we have that refer to the eyes: 'he eyeballed me', 'she really opened my eyes', 'he has shifty eyes', 'she gave him the eye'.

Gazing

We are enthralled by other people's eyes. When we first see someone or look at a picture of them, our gaze goes first to the eyes.

Next, we scan their face. In social situations, we repeatedly gaze at the triangular area between the eyes and the mouth.

When we look at someone's face, the first place our eyes go to is the area around their eyes...

and their mouth.

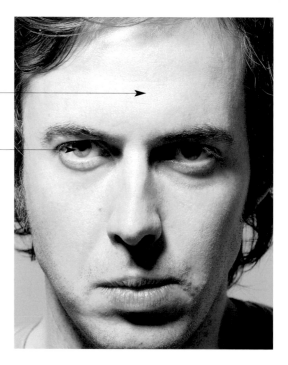

A direct gaze towards the eyes and forehead can be a signal of aggression...

or it may show sexual attraction between two people.

In very intimate situations, the gaze scans the area between the eyes and the chest. The gaze also may drop down to the crotch and back up again to the face.

A great deal of unconscious signalling comes through eye contact. How long you spend 'eye to eye' with another person indicates how well you know that person and how well you are getting on with them. It is a signal of attention, interest and interaction, as well as an indicator of our attitudes and emotions.

Eye contact can be short or long, direct or indirect or interrupted. Different cultures have different rules about the length of time we can gaze into someone's eyes. These rules are also influenced by age, gender, status and how friendly we are with the other person.

Scanning the area from the eyes to the chest happens in intimate and sexual situations.

The Pupils

Enlarged or dilated pupils mean we are looking at something or someone we like.

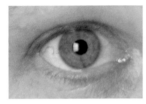

Beady, small or contracted pupils mean we are looking at something we don't like.

We prefer to be friends with people with large pupils, but we can't control the size of our pupils consciously.

Here are some of the basics of eye contact in Western cultures.

Direct eye contact

Direct eye contact is a signal of sincerity, trustworthiness and open and truthful communication. People using direct eye contact are also seen as confident: they 'look us in the eye'.

Staring or overusing direct eye contact is considered aggressive, threatening, unsettling and rude. This is true across cultures. Only young children are allowed to stare openly without it being taken the wrong way. It can also mean aggression or a direct challenge: the origin of the expression 'eyeball to eyeball'. The difference in meaning is apparaent is in the pupils of the eyes: with attraction the other person will have large pupils; with aggression or intimidation the pupils will be small and constricted.

To tell someone off and show off your control and power, look the person directly in the eyes.

As a rule of thumb, to make sure a conversation keeps on a friendly tack, maintain direct eye contact for about two-thirds of the conversation.

Frequent eye contact

Women use more eye contact than men. It signals their interest and involvement. Men use eye contact to signal power, dominance and authority.

You are more likely to look at the other person if you are an extrovert, if you like them, are attracted to them or interested in them. Also, you are more likely to look at the other person if you are interested in the topic of conversation or if you are trying to get a response.

Infrequent eye contact:

Avoiding a lot of eye contact is a signal of insecurity, sadness, shame, embarrassment, dishonesty or disinterest. If someone doesn't meet your eyes or their eyes continually shift away (shifty eyes), it means they're not comfortable with the other person or it's a difficult topic.

You are less likely to look at the other person if you are of a lower status, introverted, depressed or you don't like them.

When speaking, you make less eye contact than when you listen. The exception is in public presentations when the presenter consciously makes frequent eye contact with the audience.

WATCH OUT

Be suspicious of the other person's honesty if he does not meet your gaze for around one-third of the conversation.

Breaking eye contact

▸ **Eye dips:** Looking away and lowering the eyes is seen as being shy, sad or submissive.

▸ **Sideways glances:** Glancing from the side shows flirtatious interest if it goes with a smile and a eyebrow raise, but criticism if accompanied by a frown or a down-turned mouth.

▸ **Eye block:** Some people block the eyes by blinking for a fraction longer than normal. This is a signal that they have lost interest or are feeling negative.

▸ **Broken gaze:** When you break your gaze, you will consistently look away to the left or right. Breaking to the left is thought to signify a high artistic imagination; to the right is thought to signify a more scientific personality and lower visual imagination.

---

must know

Cultural differences

Direct eye gazing is considered rude in many cultures; in others it carries a sexual meaning. If you are travelling or are on business in another country, remember that the reason someone avoids catching your eye may be because it is considered offensive to look directly at you.

Here are some cultural differences:

▷ Many Asians, especially the Japanese, find too much direct eye contact to be intimidating.

▷ The same is true of Puerto Ricans and Native Americans. Too much eye contact may be seen as a sexual invitation.

▷ Raising an eyebrow in the Philippines is a greeting.

▷ In Thailand, eye contact is very important in social interaction.

▷ Muslim women in many cultures will avoid direct eye contact with men.

Other uses of the eyes

Eye use is not just restricted to gazing and making eye contact. The lowering and raising of the eyelids and eyebrows, the widening and narrowing of the eyes and other eye movements can all be used effectively to convey various messages.

Eyebrows

Lowering your eyebrows makes you look more confrontational. It can also be a sign of anger.

You can raise your eyebrows to show you're not a threat, that you don't believe something or that you're interested in the conversation. Raised eyebrows combined with a shrug and normal-size eyes signals submission. On the other hand, raising one eyebrow looks quizzical, knowing or curious – think of Roger Moore. Groucho Marx used the exaggerated raising and lowering of fake eyebrows to emphasize his jokes and underline punchlines. These are known as eyebrow flutters.

Having wide eyes with the eyebrows in a normal position is a signal of anger. Wide eyes with raised eyebrows signals fear.

Eye movements

There are a great variety of eye movements. Winking is one deliberate way to signal something to another person – in this case friendliness or light-heartedness. Eyes can be used in a more subtle way to get a response when a person wants to show they are submissive or dominant.

Submissive people move their eyes rapidly back and forth as if they are looking for an escape route.

Raising one eyebrow makes you look curious, knowing or quizzical.

The eyes can be opened wider for a vulnerable and baby-like look.

Widening the eyes by opening them and pulling the eyelids back makes us look more baby-like, as babies have large eyes in relation to the size of their face. This effect is used to make a person look innocent, attentive and vulnerable, to disarm, or to provoke protectiveness. Princess Diana used this eye gesture regularly. Rapid eye widening is also used as a dominant gesture. Mrs Thatcher used quick 'eye flashes' consistently to underline her points.

People who narrow their eyes are also seen as dominant. Peter Collett, the Oxford psychologist and body language expert, refers to this as the 'visor eye' effect. The word 'visor' is used because it is as if the person is looking through a small slit in a helmet. Looking over the top of your glasses is similar to narrowing your eyes, and can be used as an expression of dominance.

Looking over the top of sunglasses makes you look dominant.

Eye patterns

The meaning of eye movements has been taken to a deeper level in Neuro-Linguistic Programming (NLP), created by Richard Bandler and John Grinder. NLP draws conclusions about the relationship of eye movements to a person's memory, and how they process thoughts as well as feelings. When someone moves their eyes in a certain direction, they are accessing a certain mode of thinking. These patterns seem to be true of most people.

Visual

A person accessing a visual image in their brain will move their eyes up and then to the left or right. If they move their eyes up and to their right, they are constructing an imaginary visual image, for example, 'What would my house look like if I painted it blue?' If they move their eyes up and to their left, they are remembering a visual image, for example, 'What does my bedroom look like?' You will notice speakers often do this as they try to remember the picture of the notes they memorized earlier.

This can be a good way to spot a lie. If you ask someone to remember something they have seen and they move their eyes up to their right, it is worth questioning whether they are making up a picture.

Sounds

To remember or imagine a sound, the eyes move sideways – to the left or right. If they are to the person's right, they are imagining a sound, in other words, something in the future, for example, 'What will my boss say when I ask for a pay rise?' If their eyes move to their left, they are remembering a sound. 'I remember a month ago he said he would give me a pay rise.'

Self-talk

If you move your eyes down and to your left, you are thinking generally about the world around you and trying to making sense of it all through a conversation with yourself.

Feelings

If you move your eyes down and to your right, you are accessing your feelings. You are asking yourself, 'How do I feel about this?' It is almost as if you are looking down to your stomach to find your 'gut instinct'.

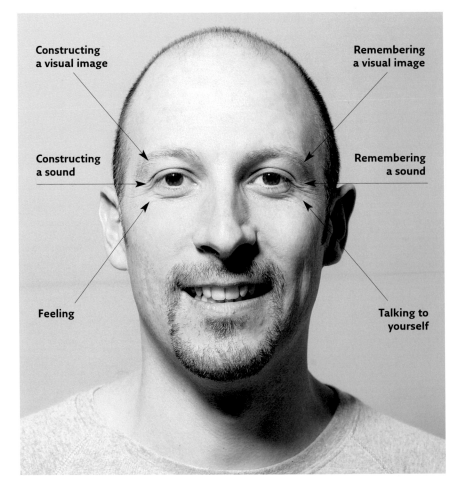

Constructing a visual image

Remembering a visual image

Constructing a sound

Remembering a sound

Feeling

Talking to yourself

The Face

There are 28 bones in the face and skull, which makes the face a very flexible and mobile communication tool. After the eyes, it is the most powerful part of the body for making nonverbal communication.

Our first impressions of another person come from their face. Of all the animals, we have the most expressive faces. The face expresses your identity and your personality.

Expressions are used for two purposes: to influence others and to express our inner feelings and opinions. They can give an overview of how positive or negative someone is and provide subtle clues as to how a person may act in the future.

Expressions

There are two types of expression: slow or sustained expressions, for example, smiles and frowns; and micro-expressions, that is, expressions that leak fleetingly across the face. Micro-expressions are hard to spot except in a slowed-down film as they may last only a quarter of a second or so. But they do reveal the true emotions behind the surface expression.

Sometimes you will spot a negative expression starting to leak through onto the face – maybe the beginnings of a frown or anger. If the person is hiding their emotions, they will try to cover them up quickly with a smile. The smile is the most commonly used mask of our real emotions.

Smile facts

Smiling shows that you are warm, friendly and approachable. Smiles can be open and wide, or closed and tight. With a slight smile, the mouth is usually closed. Open smiles show the teeth.

As you have already seen in chapter one, real smiles are symmetrical and always start in the eyes. Fake smiles, on the other hand, are made only with the mouth. They are also slightly asymmetrical and leave the face too slowly or too quickly. Fake, mouth-only smiles tend to be used by submissive people towards dominant people. They are also used when we first meet someone and are assessing them.

But be careful, if you start smiling too broadly in a business conversation, others may wonder why you're so happy. They might become suspicious and wonder whether you think you have the upper hand in the negotiation.

With a sincere smile, both sides of the face are symmetrical, and there are creases in the mouth and eyes.

With an insincere, or crocodile, smile, the face may appear asymmetrical. The smile is made with the mouth or lower half of the face, rather than with the eyes. It lasts for longer than a genuine smile.

The Head

Heads talk. They are highly expressive. People who are talking together move their heads as part of their interaction. They may move their heads forwards, backwards or tilt or cock them to the side. They may nod or shake their head, move it slowly or quickly.

Conversational heads

The head is what we usually look at during a conversation. Movements of the head are effective communicators of our mood and feelings towards other people, and they are easy to spot. Watch a group of people and notice the angle and movements of their heads.

Each speaker uses movements of the chin and slight nods when speaking to emphasize words and phrases.

Listeners tilt their heads at an angle to show attention. Women use these movements, known as head cocks, more than men. The head of the listener points towards the speaker to show to whom they are listening. The listener may unconsciously copy some of the speaker's movements to show rapport.

A third person interrupting the conversation may dip their head a little to acknowledge they are disrupting it.

Listeners may tilt or cock their head at an angle to show they are paying attention.

Nodding

The most universal head movement of nonverbal communication is the nod. Although men use nods slightly more than women, both sexes nod to show that they are listening. It is a gesture of silent agreement with the speaker. It signals understanding, acceptance and approval.

Large, slow nods mean the listener is happy for the speaker to continue speaking. Occasional nodding encourages the speaker to carry on speaking for longer. Fast nods mean the listener agrees but wants to speak soon.

Putting your heads together so that one touches the other is the head's version of a kiss. It is often used by lovers to cut out the rest of the world.

Aggressive heads If you thrust your head forwards from the shoulders, it will be taken as a threat to the person you are talking to. Thrust it forwards more and it becomes a head butt.

Thrusting the head forwards is a sign of aggression.

Putting heads together so that one touches the other is like the head's way of kissing

Other head movements

▶ **Tilts of the head** are used as greeting gestures.

▶ **Holding the head up at a slight backwards angle** can be seen as being arrogant or aggressive, or simply 'holding your head up high'.

▶ **Lowering the head** can be a submissive gesture or a sign of depression.

▶ **The head can be used to beckon** by moving it back and forth several times.

▶ **Shaking the head slightly** from side to side is a sign of reluctance.

▶ **Head swivels** are frequently used by men who have noticed an attractive woman walk past.

▶ **Tossing the head**, as a horse would toss its mane, indicates disdain. Head tosses are used more by women than men.

If you hold your head up high in a conversation, you may look arrogant.

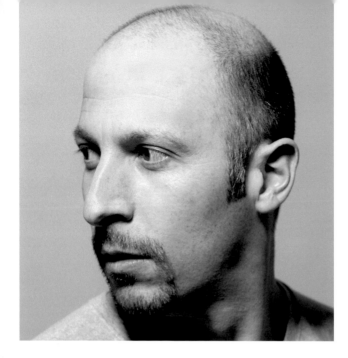

Swivelling the
head to watch an
attractive woman
walk by is something
men do frequently.

Watch out. Even
slight head shaking
in your listener can
mean that they're
not happy.

WANT TO KNOW MORE?

▷ Facial expressions
  See chapter 1
  Basics of body language
▷ Head tosses and hair
  flicks
  See chapter 8
  Attraction and dating
▷ Pupils
  See chapter 8
  Attraction and dating

3 Hands, arms and legs

Hand, arm and leg movements signal from a distance what we are thinking. We use them to create a range of deliberate and unconscious gestures: standing, sitting, waving, touching and holding. This chapter looks at the way we use gestures to enhance our repertoire of nonverbal communication.

Hands

If you clench your hands together, press your palms into each other or entwine your fingers, you are talking with each movement. Hands are the most animated and communicative part of the body we have available to us other than the face. After all, what would we do without touch? A whole area of sensory communication comes through this part of the body.

must know

The interpretation of hand movements is not a science, but there is a general consensus among researchers as to the probable meaning of many movements.

For example:
▷ If the hands are hanging down by the side of the body when sitting or standing, it is a sign that the person is either feeling relaxed and calm or listless and tired.
▷ If the hands and lower arms are moved around a lot, the person may be expressive and active or nervy and tense.
▷ If someone fidgets with their hands, chews their hands or picks at their fingernails, it is a sign that they are anxious or ill at ease.
▷ Clenching your hands into fists is a sign of frustration or anger, either with another person or yourself (see right).

Hands have always fascinated mankind. Ancient cultures even developed a series of meanings to be given to the shape of the hands and the lines on the palms. Body language research may not attribute meaning to 'what' the hands look like, but it does explain 'how' they are used.

Hand movements

Talking hands: Before man was able to speak, he needed a way to communicate about his environment, so he used his hands. Even now when an idea can be communicated through speech, this behaviour has stayed with us.

Hands are commonly used across cultures

▶ in conversation to illustrate words;

▶ as a greeting – to wave, hug or shake hands;

▶ to point out directions;

▶ or to express emotions such as anger.

When talking to another person, your hands may chop, point, jab the air, emphasize or even substitute for a word, or beat out the rhythm of your speech to illustrate and embellish your thoughts.

Our hands are also important because we appear to use them to help us think. Even if no one else is present in the room and you are thinking about a subject, you may catch yourself using your hands in some way to help the formation of an idea or to express an emotion. The next time you are speaking on the telephone, notice how many hand gestures you make.

Cultural differences: Hand movements do vary between cultures. Some cultures are very open in their movements. The Italians, for example, use their whole arms to gesture when talking. North Americans use their lower arms and hands.

Other cultures, for example in Asia, are more restrained and gesture from the wrist. In these cultures, large gestures would be seen as dominant or overexcitable. In Italy, cultures using smaller hand movements appear reserved.

The amount of movement does not reflect the amount of emotion. In Britain, we tend to think of people from Latin cultures as excitable because they move their hands and arms a lot. In fact, there is no connection between the amount of movement and the amount of emotion a person is feeling.

must know

Men and women
Women use more hand gestures than men during conversations with the opposite sex. When talking to other women, they use fewer hand gestures.

Open palms show
that you are being
open with the other
person. You are
showing them you
have nothing to hide.

Palms

An open palm facing upwards is an immediate sign
of truth and honesty. This is something we are very aware of
historically. Oaths of allegiance are taken with the open palm
over the heart. We hold our palm up to face an audience when
we swear to tell the truth.

Holding your palms out to someone shows you have no
weapon in your hands and want to be open with them. It says
'Look. I've got nothing to hide.' It is a submissive gesture and it
can be used deliberately to persuade someone of equal status
to do something for you.

Hiding your palms by tucking your hands away out of
sight may be a deliberate attempt to deceive the other person
or to lie to them.

Turning your palm down towards another person is a
dominant gesture. However, it will not go down well if the other
person considers that they are above you in status, or even if
they are of equal status.

If a salesman rubs his hands together, watch out. He may think he's about to make a lot of money from you.

Rubbing the palms together signals that you think something good is about to happen. You may spot a salesperson rubbing his hands together during negotiations with a client in anticipation of gaining a sale. Or you may rub your hands together when you are about to take part in an exciting activity or listen to an interesting talk.

Thumbs

Showing off the thumbs by poking them out of a back or front pocket is a gesture of dominance. Gesturing by pointing the thumb up indicates the same thing. If you point your thumb towards another person, it is an aggressive way to mock them and sends a negative message about what you think about them.

Hands in the pockets with the thumbs showing is a gesture of dominance.

Hand positions

Hands are highly flexible tools for us to use as we communicate. Their flexibility makes them very expressive. Watch for the signals that are used to accompany speech and to substitute for words. Notice, too, how eloquent your own hands are.

Steepling the hands so that the fingers and thumbs are lightly pressed together and the palms are separate is often used when speaking.

Still hands

Hand steeples: When the hands are steepled, the tips of the fingers of each hand are pressed together, almost as if in prayer, to form a steeple shape. The hands are either pointing up or down, and the palms are kept separate.

This gesture may occur in a cluster of gestures or by itself. It is often used by dominant individuals who are talking to people of lower status. If the hands are pointed upwards, the person is likely to be speaking to another person. If they are listening, the fingers are more likely to be pointed down.

This is a gesture of self-assurance or, at least, of someone who is deliberately trying to look confident. If it is combined with a lifted-up chin, it can look arrogant.

One hand gripping the other hand behind the back is a gesture often used by members of the Royal Family and other authority figures like teachers.

Clenched hands: Hands that are clasped together in front of a person signal negativity or frustration.

They may rest on a table, be held in front of the face or in front of the body.

A hand may also be used to grip the other hand behind the back. This is a sign of dominance, as the person using the gesture feels confident enough not to protect their front with their arms. Members of the Royal Family often walk with their hands in this position, as do authority figures such as police officers and teachers.

Hand and wrist grips: Gripping the wrist with the hand behind the back is different. It is a signal that the person is trying to keep control of themselves and that they are frustrated. If the hand grips the arm further up behind the body, the person may be experiencing a stronger emotion. Holding your hands in front of your crotch in a fig-leaf gesture is a defensive signal.

One hand gripping the wrist of the other hand may signal frustration.

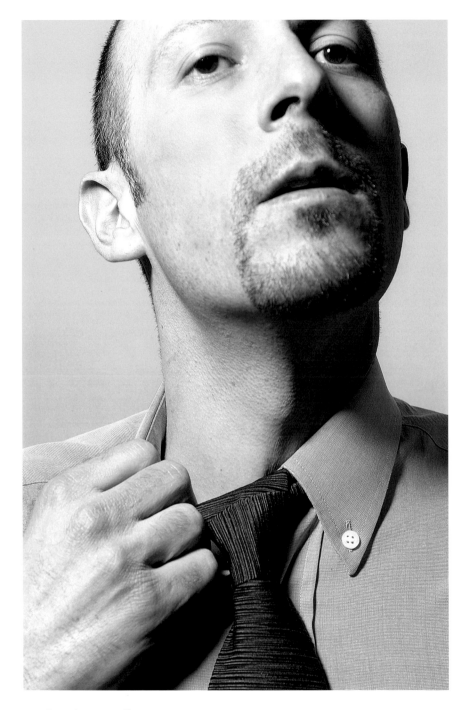

Moving hands

Fingers: If a finger is raised while someone else is speaking, it is a sign that they may want to interrupt and speak. If the finger is raised only slightly, it may be taken as a signal that the person is not very sure of themselves. If it is raised decisively, it means that the person is dominant and is issuing a threat.

Finger and thumb rubs indicate to another person that you are expecting money from them.

Hand to face gesture

Mouth cover: Covering the mouth with the hand may indicate deceit. It is as if, by covering the mouth, you are using the hand to guard against letting out the truth. However, putting your fingers in your mouth mimics the action of a baby sucking its mother's breast, and shows that the person needs comfort and reassurance.

Ear, eye and neck rubs: Rubbing the ear with the hand may gesture doubt or deceit. Rubbing the eye is used in the same way. It is as if you don't want to see someone else's lie, or if you are telling a lie, you don't want to see the person's reaction to your lie.

Rubbing the neck can be a sign of frustration, while scratching the neck signals uncertainty. Rubbing the neck specifically at the back or pulling on a collar can indicate lying. It is almost as if lying causes the neck to become itchy or painful. Hitting the back of the head then rubbing the neck is a sign of frustration with yourself or someone else.

Chin: Stroking the chin slowly with the hand indicates that a person is evaluating and thinking about what is being said. When they rest a closed hand on the chin, it also signals that they are contemplating or evaluating what is being said. But, if you see someone resting their hands on their chin and supporting the whole head, it is a sign that they are bored or tired and may be trying to stop themselves from falling asleep.

Pulling on a shirt collar may be a sign of discomfort or that the person is lying.

Arms and legs

The way you position your arms and legs is a clear signal of how relaxed or tense you are. One of the first things you can spot from a distance is how open or closed a person is being with their body language by how they have placed their limbs.

Barriers

We all put up barriers between ourselves and others if we do not feel positive towards them for some reason – we may not like them or we may feel defensive towards them. If there is something we can use as a physical barrier, like a piece of furniture or a handbag, we do. If not, then we use our bodies.

Folding your arms may be a defensive gesture (though as an isolated gesture it may simply mean you are cold). Crossing your legs tightly into your body is also a negative sign.

Legs crossed at the ankles is a subtle barrier between one person and another.

Grasping hold of the other arm across the chest is a disguised arm barrier.

Arm barriers

These barrier gestures may be disguised. For example, one arm may be used instead of two. The most common barriers are where you fold your arms tightly across the chest, or grip the opposite arm. One arm may be held in front of the body, grasping hold of the opposite arm or holding a shirt cuff, glass of water or watch. You may also clench your fists.

Leg barriers

Legs are used in the same way. If they are combined with crossed arms, then be doubly aware.

Legs may be crossed one over the other while sitting (this is generally right over left). When standing, legs are likely to be crossed at the ankles. This may be a signal that the person is holding back emotionally. They may feel nervous. Interviewees often cross their ankles during an interview.

While sitting, one foot may lock around the opposite leg. This can be a sign of shyness. However, a more aggressive position that reveals the crotch is the leg lock, where one leg is crossed and rests on the opposite thigh.

Pointing

Pointing with the feet or knees shows how a person is thinking about another person in the room.

When sitting, if you cross your legs and your knees point towards someone, that is the person you are most interested in. This may be a sexual interest or simply the person you like the most. If they feel the same towards you, their body language will be the same.

Your body does not necessarily follow the direction of the pointer. It may well be that you are talking to one person but the person that interests you is in a different part of the room. Subconsciously, though, they may see you and pick up the signal.

The feet and knees do not have to point towards a person. They may point towards an exit if you are feeling uncomfortable in a particular situation.

WANT TO KNOW MORE?

▷ **Handshakes**
 See chapter 6
 Meeting and greeting
▷ **Arm and leg barriers**
 See chapter 9
 Negativity
▷ **Pointing**
 See chapter 8
 Attraction

4 Body and touch

How you position your body – through standing, sitting, kneeling, squatting or lying down; the angle of the back and torso; and how stiff or relaxed you are – communicates and also affects how you feel. Even a long way away from another person, you can begin to form an impression about them.

The Body

Watch someone walk into a room. Are they slumping? Are they stiff or rigid? Is their back straight? You will without doubt draw conclusions about their level of confidence: do they feel self-confident or shy and insecure? How relaxed do they feel? Are they powerful or weak? Are they open or defensive?

Posture

Mention posture and it might bring to mind well-brought-up Victorian girls in deportment classes walking around with books on their heads. What posture means in body language terms is how we use and move our bodies to experience and convey emotion.

The advantage of posture is that it is a form of nonverbal communication that is very visible even when you are not at close quarters to the other person. You may not be able to see from a distance whether two people having a conversation at a party are smiling at each other or grimacing, but it is easy to see how laid-back or erect their posture is.

Posture and personality

Posture changes according to people's moods and their relationships. However, you will notice that certain personalities habitually adopt a particular posture.

People who feel confident or in charge hold their bodies erect. Those who are of a low status or often feel depressed or shy tend to walk around with lowered heads, a humped posture and slumped or rounded shoulders.

Research has found that unconfident and depressed people can be taught to feel better about themselves by consistently standing up straight and correcting their postures to eliminate slumping. There are added benefits, too. Walking around with an erect posture brings clearer thinking and a broader observation of what is going on around you, and it should provoke a more positive reaction from other people. If you keep an erect, confident posture, you will find people accept your point of view more readily than if you look submissive.

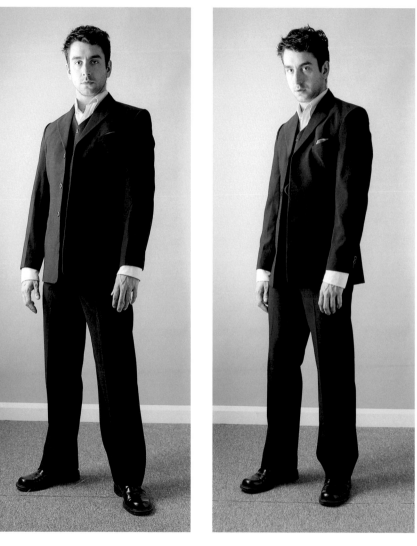

Confident people stand tall and erect, and provoke a more positive reaction from others.

Slumping, bending and lowering the head may show a lower status or depression.

Placing the hands on the hips looks aggressive.

Common postures

Different postures reflect different internal emotions. Confidence breeds an erect posture but it works the other way around as well. Adopt an erect posture, keep your shoulders straight, stomach in and hold your head up high, and you will look confident and begin to feel it, too.

Standing with an erect but stiff posture appears tense and defensive, while an erect upper body with relaxed shoulders looks open and self-assured.

Want to appear and feel weaker and less confident? Drop your head down and slump. Fold your arms in front of your chest and you'll look unsympathetic or negative.

Leaning changes the way you are seen. If you lean forwards, you'll look interested and positive. Lean back and you will look disinterested or negative.

If two people adopt the same position, mirroring the angle of each other's spine it is a sign of rapport. It means they are friends, lovers or just getting on very well and finding things in common.

Walking

To look confident, walk briskly with an erect upper torso, head held high, and let your arms swing in a relaxed, open manner.

Watch how American presidents do it. They try to look like fit, healthy young men by striding purposefully forwards.

Their arms swing across the body, turning slightly inwards to produce a macho, muscular effect.

Status and power

How much space you occupy in a room indicates how powerful you are in relation to others in the room. If you are standing while the other people are sitting, you will be seen as authoritative, providing they accept that your status is superior to theirs. If they perceive you as their equal or their inferior, you will be taken as 'uppity' or arrogant.

A calm, relaxed and confident sitting posture.

A tense, nervous, low self-esteem posture.

Touch

Touching is a deliberate bodily contact between two people. The experience of being touched by another person, even accidentally, can provoke positive and negative emotions. The skin is the largest part of the body, accounting for 15 per cent of the body's weight. It is sensitive to temperature and pressure. Even the lightest touch is felt deeply and can send a message about attraction, sympathy, approval or relative power.

Impact of touch

How much we want to touch or be touched by another person relates to how much we like them. Touching can lead us to like someone else but only if it feels natural.

Researchers tested the impact of touch. They asked two sets of speakers to tell another person a story. The first set of speakers told the story simply in words, standing away from the listener. The second group of speakers told the same story in the same way but touched the listener for a second on their arm at important points in the story.

When the listeners were asked afterwards what they thought about the speakers, they rated the second group as better story-tellers. They also liked them more as people. Significantly, the second set of listeners also remembered more of the story than the first group.

Touching rules

The amount of touching a person is comfortable with depends partly on how much their family hugged, kissed and touched each other. Be careful if you don't know someone well, though. There are complex rules about where we can touch people on their bodies, how long we can touch them for, how heavily or lightly we can touch them and with what part of our body we can touch them.

Many Western cultures read sexual meanings into touch, so if you get it wrong, you will be in trouble.

Touch and status

In a relationship between two people, the person who has more power and status can touch the person with lower status, but not vice versa. You're more likely to touch someone you're giving an order to than receiving an order from.

An extreme example of this can be seen with the Queen and her family. There are strict rules about touching a member of the Royal Family. When the Queen is in public, it is she who decides whether or not to shake someone's hand, for example. Touching the 'Royal Person' is not allowed, which is why there was such a storm in the media when the Australian Prime Minister Paul Keating put his hand on the Queen's back during a Royal visit.

The secret love affair between Princess Margaret and Group Captain Peter Townsend was revealed when she unthinkingly touched his jacket in public, immediately revealing the closeness of their relationship. Princess Diana often touched people in public, particularly those who were ill or hurt in some way, and great significance was placed on this by the media.

Touching a member of the Royal Family is a breach of status rules. The Spice Girls touched Prince Charles with unspoken permission at the height of their fame.

Cigarettes
▷ People disguise their anxiety by smoking.
▷ Holding a cigarette is like touching a security blanket. It is an alternative to touching your face directly with your hands for self-comfort.
▷ Sucking a cigarette is also an unconscious and stress-relieving oral reminder of suckling your mother's breast.

Smoking a cigarette disguises anxiety.

Building relationships

Touch can be used to signal interest and involvement during interaction with another person. People are most likely to touch each other when they want to express support and sympathy, ask for help, try to win someone round to their way of thinking, or give advice.

Self-touch and anxiety

Tense people touch themselves frequently as a means of comforting and consoling themselves. This is often done unconsciously.

Notice how stressed people often rub and massage their hands, hold their arms and wrists, scratch, pinch and rub their skin, tug their earlobes and comb their fingers through their hair. By stimulating or itching the skin, you release pain receptors that send positive feelings to the brain.

This form of behaviour illustrates how similar we are to apes. Apes can often be seen scratching themselves when they are in a group setting and feel threatened.

When people are stressed, the parts of the body that they touch most frequently are the head, face and hair. These are the places where a mother touches her baby to console it. As an adult, being comforted by your mother in this way is inappropriate, so you mimic her actions.

Touching objects

Anxious people also use external objects as comforters. If you watch students waiting for an exam to start, some of them may suck the ends of their spectacles or chew the end of a pencil. Others may chew their fingernails, even suck their thumbs like a baby.

Self-touch is a sign of stress and tension.

Courting

When men and women are trying to attract each other, they use self-touch to show off parts of their bodies, for example, by running their fingers through their hair as a means of display. They also touch external objects, for example, a woman will stroke the stem of a wine glass to prompt the man unconsciously to think about her doing the same to him in the future.

Finally, they touch each other. Even in the early stages of an attraction, touch will inadvertently, or accidentally, occur. This is normally initiated by the man, though it is the woman who first signals that she is willing to be approached by him.

Men and women

There are also differences between how much men and women touch in social situations. It appears that women are more sensitive to touch than men,

A couple hand in hand may be family members or in love.

must know

Cultural differences
▷ In Latin cultures, more touching is acceptable in the workplace than in Britain and North America. Men regularly greet their colleagues with a handshake. Men and women may greet each other with a kiss.
▷ In many Arab countries, it is normal to touch each other in work by, for example, taking your colleague's arm to guide them.
▷ Most Asian cultures avoid public shows of affection. However, in China, the Philippines and Korea, friends of the same sex often walk hand in hand, and everyone expects to push and shove in a queue without apologizing.
▷ In Japan, people try to keep their personal space and not touch in queues, unless they are forced to because of a large crowd.

Are they are in love?

and they use touch as a sign of love more than men. They touch more when saying 'hello' or 'goodbye' than men, and are happier to be touched by a stranger.

Generally, men initiate more touch than women. However, this changes in old age when women begin to touch more than men.

With children, girls are touched by their parents more often than boys. Even children, though, avoid too much touching of children of the opposite sex.

Teenagers are more likely to touch each other when boys and girls are both present, rather than if only one sex is present.

WANT TO KNOW MORE?

▷ **Hugs and kisses**
   See chapter 6
   Meeting and greeting
▷ **Personal space**
   See Introduction
▷ **Touching**
   See chapter 8
   Attraction

WHITE WINES:
SAN RAFAEL CHARDONNAY CHILE 2004
PALENA SAUVIGNON BLANC CHILE 2004
SPY VALLEY SAUVIGNON BLANC N.Z. 2003
CLAUDE MICHOT POUILLY FUMÉ FRANCE 2003
RED WINES:
CÔTE À CÔTE ROUGE FRANCE 2003
LA SERRE SYRAH
SPY VALLEY PINOT
VEUVE CLICQUOT

5 Territory and personal space

Space speaks. Just as countries have borders and territory, humans have personal space with rules about who can enter it. There are different rules for private and public space, for different countries and cultures, work and personal life, for men and women.

Territory

How often does a stranger walk into your home, have a bath, help himself to food or sit in your favourite chair and start watching television? Presumably not very often. Unless he's a burglar or a madman, he will recognize he has no right to be there.

Like animals or countries, we will fight for our territories, and grieve if they are threatened or violated. We do not have the freedom to stand, sit or go where we want without impacting on other people.

The body language we use reflects this, and it depends on where we are and our feelings of ownership towards a particular space. Stand too close and you could be invading someone's territory. Stand too far away and you will be seen as unfriendly.

The rules of territory

Human beings have three basic territories in their world.

▶ **Home:** This is kept for family or people you invite in. You decorate and personalize your home to show that it belongs to you, in the same way as an animal marks its territory. If someone enters your home without an invitation, it's likely to provoke an aggressive or angry response. Each time you return home, you unconsciously walk around to 'check for invaders'. In animals this is known as reconnaissance.

▶ **Social territory:** The rules of social territory are more complicated, but even here we have some control over our surroundings. For example, a club will expect customers to be of a certain age or type, even gender. Anyone else who inadvertently strays in may face hostility.

▶ **Public territory:** No one owns public space. We may still show some negative body language if someone takes our favourite bench in the park, but we are then likely to let it go.

Parking spaces

Studies show that motorists treat their parking spaces as their territory. If it is obvious that you are waiting for someone to drive out of a parking space, it's not your imagination but they really will exit more slowly.

Even in public, we have rules about territory and will display negative body language if we feel it has been invaded.

Personal space

Edward Hall, the American anthropologist and founder of proxemics – the study of personal space – established that we all carry our own zones around with us wherever we go. These 'bubbles', which are determined culturally, define how much space we need to have between ourselves and other people in different social situations, regardless of walls, partitions or other fixed features of our environment.

Our personal bubble defines the invisible area we want to keep free of other people. We feel happiest if we can maintain control over our space.

Flexible space

People's zones are not static. They stretch or shrink according to the situation, and they exist in relation to other people. Every encounter you have with someone involves choices about space. How big the distance is between people is a signal about the intimacy of their relationship, their relative status and their gender. It tells both the people inside the interaction, as well as outside observers, about the relationship between the participants.

The intimate zone (15–45cm/6–18in) is for people who are happy to touch and be touched.

The four zones

Hall defined four zones that apply to people in Europe, the USA and Canada:

▶ **The intimate zone (0-45cm/ 0-18in):** This is reserved for people you are happy to touch or be touched by. Intrusions into this zone are generally experienced as unpleasant, disturbing, if not threatening. This zone is used for contacts such as sex or contact sports.

▶ **The personal zone (45cm-1.2m/ 18in-4ft):** The personal zone is kept for family members and close personal friends. In this zone, you are at arm's length from another person and can shake hands easily.

▶ **The social-consultative zone (1.2-3.6m/4-12ft):** This is an impersonal zone. Most social and business contacts take place in this zone. Touch is not possible. A lot of verbal communication is used.

▶ **The public zone (3.6m+/12ft +):** This is a formal zone. You are not trying to interact with other people but more likely trying to ignore them. For example, look where strangers sit when they go to a beach. Displays of nonverbal gestures are used, as the distances are too great for normal level of verbal communication.

The personal zone (45cm-1.2m/18in-4ft) is reserved for family members and close friends.

The social zone (1.2-3.6m/4-12ft) is an impersonal zone where touch is not possible.

The public zone (3.6m+/12ft+) is a formal zone where social interaction is avoided.

Be very careful not to invade the personal space of others – it will lose you friends. One experiment showed that 30 per cent of people moved away within one minute when they felt that their personal space had been invaded; over half moved away within ten minutes.

Talking in comfort means observing rules of space for Persons A and B.

Invasion

Controlling who enters our space puts us in control of our privacy. If you are not getting the amount of privacy or intimacy you want, your body language will change to show negativity and coping signals. Or you may lose interest in the conversation and walk away from the other people.

Police officers and interrogators are taught to use the discomfort that invading people's personal space brings in the interrogation room. They deliberately invade a suspect's personal space to crowd them and build a sense of power. This gives them a psychological advantage over the suspect.

Rules of space

Strangers who try to come into these zones uninvited make us feel nervous. Either they have invaded our space by accident, because they don't understand the cultural rules, or they are doing it deliberately as a sexual or physically aggressive move.

When the invasion is accidental, the invader may be seen as 'pushy', meaning he's probably come into the personal zone.

Someone who stands outside the social zone may be seen as 'stand-offish'. Another may be warned out of this zone – 'to keep his distance'.

In each case, you will observe that the body language of the people around changes to reflect these attitudes.

When an uninvited person tries to stand too close, Person A feels uncomfortable.

If Person A is much bigger than Person B, he will often stand further away than normal to appear less threatening.

Influences on space

There are a number of personal, social, physical and cultural factors that can make us change our zones. Each of these factors can play a role, and there may be several influences at work at the same time.

▶ **Age:** Children and adults have very different boundaries. The size of zones increases up until you become a teenager.

▶ **Gender:** Women tend to allow people to come closer to them than men. Women also tend to allow invaders to take over their space more readily than men, who are more aggressive in their warning off the invader. But when there is an implied threat, women keep a greater distance than men. Men tend to sit or stand face to face with people they like. Women position themselves next to the person they like.

▶ **Personality:** Your personality modifies your need for space. Extraverts tend not to need as much space between them and another person as does an introvert. Mental health also appears to be a factor. A person who is over anxious will stand further away from others than someone who is relaxed.

- **Status:** The higher your status, the more space you will take up. You are also more likely to invade the space of those of lower status.

- **Height, weight and physical difference:** A very tall person will often stand further away from others in a conversation. This is probably so as not to appear overdominant or overpowering. A very heavy person is more likely to keep a slightly greater distance from others, as is someone who is disfigured in some way.

- **Focus of the conversation:** Watch someone tell a secret and automatically move closer to the other person. Any third person who walks in will either stand away at a distance or give an apology.

- **The context of an interaction:** The amount of noise and light, the temperature and how much space is available all influence how far people distance themselves from each other.

- **Attraction and similarity:** Women stand nearer to men they're attracted to. Men don't show their attraction by changing their position in the same way. Experiments on couples with similar personalities show they stand closer together on a first date than dissimilar couples.

It is acceptable to move closer to a person when sharing a secret.

Town versus Country

How much personal space you need is influenced by the population density of the area where you grew up. If you were raised in the country with few other people around, you will need more personal space than someone who grew up in a heavily populated urban environment. According to body language expert Allan Pease:

▷ Country people may have personal zones of 100cm+ (3ft) and will shake hands from further away than people in a town.
▷ Town people may have personal zones of only 45cm (18in) and will shake hands at close quarters.
▷ People from remote country areas may have personal zones of up to 1.8m (6ft). A common greeting is likely to be a hail or wave from a distance.

Country people keep a greater distance when meeting and greeting than people in the town.

Town people have smaller personal zones than people in the country and shake hands at close quarters.

Homes

How we arrange our homes reflects a complicated interplay of personal and social space. Some rooms in the home are 'open to the public'. We invite guests in as well as family members. However, we also have rooms that are very private and may be off-limits even to our close family.

Home seating

We generally have one social gathering place within the home. This is often the kitchen or the room with a dining table in it. Here we like to sit face-to-face to promote eye-to-eye contact and a close family atmosphere.

The room in which we watch TV is not always the best place for promoting a family atmosphere because the furniture is often arranged in relation to our viewing habits, rather than conversation.

The shape of the main table in the home provides clues to the relationships within a family. Round tables promote a relaxed family atmosphere. Square tables, on the other hand, are unlikely to promote the same openness.

Cultural differences

Personal zones vary between different cultures. There are different rules for space in business, dating and conversation.

Contact cultures

In 'contact cultures', for example, in France, Italy, Turkey and some Arab and Latin American cultures, there is more touch between people and they interact at closer distances.

Non-contact cultures

'Non-contact' cultures such as in Britain, Scandinavia, Austria and Germany, as well as China, India, Indonesia, Japan, Pakistan, the Philippines and Thailand, are more reserved and people keep a greater distance between each other.

Differences

► The personal 'bubbles' of the French, Greeks and Hispanics are slightly smaller than those of North Americans.

► The British, Swedish and Swiss are similar to North Americans. Their average interpersonal distance is 'arm length' – about the length of an extended arm. At the same time, they use eye contact to show involvement and interest.

► Compared with these nationalities, Russians have small interpersonal distances; they can touch each other at 'wrist length' with the wrist of an extended arm.

► Japanese need only around a 25cm (10in) personal zone. A northern European or North American might well feel their space was being invaded in a conversation with a Japanese person, but the Japanese avoid touch in social interactions.

► A Japanese man will bow and make a gesture with one hand held vertically in front of the nose to show he's about to cross someone's space. This has been described as being like the prow of a ship cutting through water.

Town people have smaller personal zones than people in the country and shake hands at close quarters.

Homes

How we arrange our homes reflects a complicated interplay of personal and social space. Some rooms in the home are 'open to the public'. We invite guests in as well as family members. However, we also have rooms that are very private and may be off-limits even to our close family.

Home seating

We generally have one social gathering place within the home. This is often the kitchen or the room with a dining table in it. Here we like to sit face-to-face to promote eye-to-eye contact and a close family atmosphere.

The room in which we watch TV is not always the best place for promoting a family atmosphere because the furniture is often arranged in relation to our viewing habits, rather than conversation.

The shape of the main table in the home provides clues to the relationships within a family. Round tables promote a relaxed family atmosphere. Square tables, on the other hand, are unlikely to promote the same openness.

must know

Lifts

▷ Even in a lift that is stuffed full of people, we keep our personal space as much as we possibly can.

▷ The first two people to walk into an empty lift will stand by the walls.

▷ The next person in will take a corner of the lift.

▷ If there are five or more people in the lift, everyone will face the door, not touch each other, watch the floor indicator and protect their bodies with their bags in a fig-leaf position.

▷ If you want to cause tension, walk into a crowded lift and face the crowd rather than the door.

The first person to board a train is most likely to sit at one end of a bench seat. The second person sits a distance away, and the third goes to the far end of the seat.

Public space

How often does a stranger sit next to you on an empty bus? Or put their towel next to yours on a beach? Or sit next to you in a restaurant and start eating your food? It would seem very odd if anyone did any of these things.

Where we sit or stand in public situations follows an instinctive and elaborate set of rules. When we are in a crowded place in public, we tend to make ourselves smaller to avoid touching other people. The exception to this is in a situation like a theatre, cinema or concert, where we tolerate less space because of our focus on the event.

Public transport and space

In some situations, such as on a crowded train or bus, strangers are forced to touch each other. Ordinarily, this would cause an anxiety response. However, if you watch how people react to each other in such situations, they tend to preserve their privacy by standing or sitting still, ignoring other people, using props such as newspapers to avoid catching other people's eyes, keeping a blank expression, making no meeting or greeting signals and looking at the floor, door or ceiling.

Public seating

In a room in a public building, people try to sit at least 2m (6ft) away from each other. If about two-thirds of the seats in a room are already taken, new people coming into the room will often leave, rather than sit down and compromise their personal space.

Research shows that in a library or cafeteria, for example, people choose to sit at any unoccupied tables first. The most popular tables are by the wall or in a corner of the room.

When a person comes into a busy environment and has no option but to sit at a table with one other person, they will choose to sit as far away from the other person as possible. If they are forced to be close, they would prefer to sit back-to-back, rather than side-by-side.

Such closeness tends to force conversation. When two people sit down next to each other, they often begin talking.

There are gender differences in the way we react to the person sitting near us. Men react most negatively to someone who sits opposite them at their table. Women are most negative towards an invader who sits right next to them.

Cultural differences

Personal zones vary between different cultures. There are different rules for space in business, dating and conversation.

Contact cultures

In 'contact cultures', for example, in France, Italy, Turkey and some Arab and Latin American cultures, there is more touch between people and they interact at closer distances.

Non-contact cultures

'Non-contact' cultures such as in Britain, Scandinavia, Austria and Germany, as well as China, India, Indonesia, Japan, Pakistan, the Philippines and Thailand, are more reserved and people keep a greater distance between each other.

Differences

▶ The personal 'bubbles' of the French, Greeks and Hispanics are slightly smaller than those of North Americans.

▶ The British, Swedish and Swiss are similar to North Americans. Their average interpersonal distance is 'arm length' – about the length of an extended arm. At the same time, they use eye contact to show involvement and interest.

▶ Compared with these nationalities, Russians have small interpersonal distances; they can touch each other at 'wrist length' with the wrist of an extended arm.

▶ Japanese need only around a 25cm (10in) personal zone. A northern European or North American might well feel their space was being invaded in a conversation with a Japanese person, but the Japanese avoid touch in social interactions.

▶ A Japanese man will bow and make a gesture with one hand held vertically in front of the nose to show he's about to cross someone's space. This has been described as being like the prow of a ship cutting through water.

Bowing is very common in Japan. Different levels of bow are used to show relative status.

- ▶ The Chinese allow some casual touching in a similar situation, as do people from India.
- ▶ The Japanese and Koreans feel uncomfortable with the amount of direct eye contact a Western person uses in social interactions. In Korea, a young person who uses direct eye contact with an older person is seen as being defiant or rude.
- ▶ Arabs of the same gender, use more touch, have more direct eye contact and stand at a closer distance when talking.
- ▶ These cross-cultural differences in personal space show the potential pitfalls for diplomats, tourists and anyone doing business in a foreign country. If you are not aware of different concepts of space, you may develop false assumptions about different cultures and their attitudes, causing misunderstandings, offence or anger.

WANT TO KNOW MORE?

▷ Ownership gestures
See chapter 7
Getting on well

▷ Personal space
See chapter 11
Power and domination

▷ Attraction
See chapter 8
Attraction and dating

6 Meeting, greeting and saying goodbye

The way people greet and say goodbye to each other is very specific to the culture they are in. The gestures they use acknowledge they understand the cultural rules of the other person and are prepared to enter into a relationship or interaction with them. This chapter examines how we meet people and bid them farewell.

Meeting and greeting

People from the same culture meeting each other share a set of rules about what gestures it is appropriate for them to make when they greet each other. These gestures are determined by how well the people already know each other.

There are three different stages to greeting another person. These are defined by psychologist Peter Collett as, first when you notice the other person, then going towards them and finally when you make some kind of greeting.

Greeting gestures show you have recognized each other, you are willing to approach and be friendly (or at least not be hostile) and, finally, you are willing to meet and establish the intimacy of the relationship you have with each other.

1 Noticing the other person

When you first see someone you have seen before, you use a cluster of gestures to show how happy you are to see them again.

Formal and informal situations differ. In a formal situation with someone who is an acquaintance but on an equal level with you socially, you show you have noticed them by smiling, raising the eyebrows slightly (eyebrow flash), hailing them, waving your hands and nodding or tilting the head slightly. The eyebrow flash is a gesture that seems to be used in most countries, except Japan.

With a good friend you haven't seen for a while and who is of equal status, you show recognition by using bigger gestures, such as an open mouth and a smile, waving, eyebrow flashes and widening of the eyes. It's an expression that says 'What a surprise. I'm so happy/excited to see you.'

Tilting the head and raising the eyebrows are signals of recognition.

Sometimes one of the people will signal their intention at this point to embrace the other person by stretching out their arms. They may also blow a kiss.

Smiling shows that
you are pleased to
see the other person.

Waving: Recognition is often accompanied by a hail or wave. Forms of waving or hailing – raising an arm or hand – varies from country to country but essentially they are universal gestures. In a hail, you show your open palm and offer your intention to touch the other person, even though they are out of reach. It is also thought that, historically, this evolved to show that you are not carrying a weapon.

2 Moving towards the other person

Once you have acknowledged that you both know each other, you move towards each other to make a greeting.

In a formal situation, each person walks slowly towards the other. They may look away slightly to create some distance. They may also use self-touch or arm barriers.

These signals confirm that the relationship is not a close or intimate one.

In a close relationship, in contrast, each person walks quickly, eager to reach the other. They keep looking at each other, with open body language and no defensive or protective gestures.

Strangers
Greeting gestures help us to establish relationships quickly and to transform strangers into acquaintances or friends. This is useful for our emotional well-being, as 90 per cent of us have some negative response to strangers. When meeting a stranger, you are likely to frown, bite your lip, show your tongue tip, avert your gaze and touch your own hands, body or head. These are all signs of negativity and stress.

3 Greeting

Common greetings: There are three common forms of greeting.

▶ **Handshake**
▶ **Hugging and embracing**
▶ **Kissing**

The greeting that is likely to be used will have been indicated in the body language when the two people have moved towards each other. These are symmetrical greetings, meaning that both people perform the same action at the same time.

The first few minutes of meeting someone after a break involves touching and smiling to show pleasure and as a signal that you are making up for time lost when you did not see each other. After this brief period has past, the touching is complete until you separate and another ritual takes place.

A handshake is a common greeting signal in many countries.

- ▷ In Arabic-speaking countries, the salaam is still used as a form of greeting. The right hand is brought to the chest, then to the forehead and, finally, to the side with the palm facing the other person.
- ▷ In India and Nepal, the namaste is the common greeting. The palms of the hands are placed together as if in prayer and held in front of the chest. The person bows slightly.
- ▷ The Japanese use bowing as a standard greeting, and different gradients of bow are an indication of differing levels of status in business and gender. The lower-status person bows first and for longer. The hands are placed on the knees, and the body is kept lower than the higher status person's bow – generally at around 30 degrees.

The namaste, where the palms of the hands are placed together as in prayer, is the usual greeting in India and Nepal.

Formal greetings: There are also formal forms of greeting that we seldom use now in the West, but that historically convey respect for someone of higher status:

- ▶ **Removing and doffing your hat**
- ▶ **Saluting**
- ▶ **Bowing**
- ▶ **Curtseying**
- ▶ **Genuflecting or prostrating yourself in front of another person**

These formal greetings all involve lowering your body or some part of your body in front of the other person. They are often asymmetrical greetings – only one of you performs the action. This signals that you consider yourself to be subordinate. In these situations, the other person would normally not change their position in response, which acknowledges their superiority.

One situation in which the bow and curtsey is still used is when meeting royalty. In our egalitarian Western society, it is one of the few occasions when we allow this stark status distinction.

Handshakes

Handshakes are used to say hello, goodbye, to seal a contract or to express congratulations. The handshake was originally a European convention, although other cultures have also traditionally touched the hands and other parts of the body of the person they are meeting.

The importance of handshakes

Diplomats shake hands, politicians from opposite parties shake hands, business people shake hands. Secret fraternities shake hands.

Why is a handshake so important? It seems it is a ritual of good intent, as if any transaction or interaction that it forms a part of is sealed by an intention of fair dealing and equality. Thus, candidates for the American presidency always start off their debates by shaking each other's hands, boxers touch their gloved hands before a fight, and shaking hands on a business deal used to mean a binding contract. Allowing someone into your intimate zone of personal space is a symbol of trust. Showing your open palm, as in the hail, also shows that you are not carrying a weapon.

However, within the ritual there is room for subtlety. Types of handshake vary, and even one lasting only seconds allows significant room for interpreting the personality and state of mind of each person, as well as the relationship between the two people. You can discover who is dominant and who is submissive, who is sincere or who is tense, indifferent or detached.

Main types of handshake

▶ **The Firm Handshake:** This is the handshake that all business people and leaders are taught to do. The hands are on a level and pumped two or three times with a grip that is neither too tight nor too loose. Extraverts tend to use a firm handshake, and this handshake feels open and self-confident. Women who use this handshake are thought of as being more intellectual and open to new experiences than those with a weaker handshake.

A Firm Handshake is the most acceptable handshake for business.

▶ **The Dominant Handshake:** This is a handshake used to set up control. You show dominance by keeping your palm down in relation to the other person. The hand on top is the one in control. If someone tries to shake your hand in this way and you want to wrong-foot them, literally do that. Step towards the other person with your left foot, then bring your right leg forward, too, and invade his personal space. This allows you to straighten out the hand or to turn it over, so his hand is in the submissive position.

A Dominant Handshake is used to try to control the other person.

▶ **The Limp/Dead-Fish Handshake:** The hand is relaxed without any control in the grasp. It feels passive and as if the other person is not involved in the transaction. If it is accompanied by sweat or clamminess, it is interpreted as nervousness and a sign of a weak person. But, in some countries, for example in West Africa, this handshake is the norm. Also, some world leaders and VIPs use this handshake to remain detached from the hundreds of people they have to shake hands with.

A Limp/Dead-Fish Handshake is not well regarded in Western business dealings.

In a Politician's Handshake, one person clasps the other person's hand with both hands.

A Flick Away Handshake is firm but the hand is pushed away at the end.

▶ **The Politician's Shake:** During this handshake, one person is trying to give the other person the impression of honesty and sincerity by using both hands to clasp the right hand of the other person, almost as if they are encasing it in a glove. In fact, this handshake often has the opposite effect and simply makes the other suspicious. A variation of this is to shake the hand with your right hand and use your left to hold the other person's forearm or neck.

▶ **The Bonecrusher:** This is a handshake where the grasp is too tight. It crushes the hand of the other person, and is often used as a deliberate show of strength or dominance.

▶ **The Hang-on:** In this handshake, the other person will not let go of your hand. The shake is firm and warm but it lasts too long, as the person wants to keep your attention and so physically hangs on to you. Generally, the person whose hand is being shaken does not pull their hand away but looks for an excuse to leave.

▶ **The Push/Flick Away:** The shake is firm and warm but at the end the person pushes or flicks your hand away in order to end the interaction. Someone who does this is controlling the agenda. Interestingly, the Queen uses a push-away gesture, presumably because of the sheer number of people she has to shake hands with.

▶ **The Straight Arm:** The initiator of this handshake extends a straight arm so that you cannot come forward into their personal space. The whole interaction takes place in your space.

The Queen uses a push-away handshake that allows her to control the length of time she holds the other person's hand.

Dominant Handshake: Person A holds Person B's shoulder while shaking hands.

▶ **The Pull:** The person who initiates this handshake uses a stiff arm to pull you into their territory. This either means that they are trying to manipulate you or, because of cultural reasons, they are used to a smaller personal space and are trying to close the gap.

▶ **The Finger Grip:** Only fingers are offered to be held by the other person. This handshake is often used by women, and lacks confidence and intimacy as a gesture.

Dominant Handshake: Person A holds Person B's elbow while shaking hands.

---

must know

Cultural differences
There are big cultural differences in handshaking rituals. One of the most important is which hand is used. In many countries, the left hand is used to clean yourself after going to the toilet, and so to offer your left hand to someone would be an insult.

Dominant Handshake: Person A holds Person B's wrist while shaking hands.

Hugging and kissing

Lovers hug each other. Family members and friends hug each other. Hugs vary between societies, cultures and contexts. They may use the whole body or part of the body. They may be accompanied by kissing, be sexual or platonic. Hugs give comfort or may simply be a form of greeting.

Hugging

The most intense form of greeting is the full embrace in which you put your arms around the other person and bring your bodies together. This is accompanied by kissing, touching, patting and smiling, as well as a lot of eye contact and sometimes even crying.

A squeeze or pat on the other person's shoulder or back tells them it is time to release and cut off the hug.

There are many variations of the hug and embrace, depending on the formality of the relationship, how long it has been since you saw the other person, cultural rules and how public or private the setting is.

Full-Body Hug

Main types of hug

There is more than one type of hug.

▶ **Full-Body Hug**: Both people bring their bodies together and embrace each other equally. This is an expression of great affection.

▶ **Half Hug**: The arms are put around each other but the bodies are kept slightly apart in order to avoid any sexual implication.

▶ **Side Hug**: This is another variation used by people who are worried about the sexual implications of embracing. The two people stand beside each other and put their arms around each other.

- **Attraction Hug:** If you want to show your attraction while hugging, you tend to move your feet and pelvis towards the other person and press into them.
- **Disinterested Hug:** On the other hand, if you are half-hearted, you tend to move your feet and pelvis away from the other person.
- **East European Politician's Hug:** We do not often see this now, but in its heyday this was a full-on bear hug, accompanied by a kiss on each cheek.

Kissing

Kissing is used universally in sexual contact. In greetings, the use of kissing varies from culture to culture. The main variations are:

- **Cheek Kiss:** Each person greets the other by kissing them on one or both cheeks. Which cheek is offered first varies depending on the country.
- **Air Kiss:** Each person greets the other by kissing towards the cheeks but missing slightly and not making physical contact.
- **Hand Kiss:** This is rare now, but once upon a time a man greeted a woman by kissing her hand.
- **Head kiss:** An older person will often greet a child by kissing them on the top of the head or on the forehead. It shows that they feel protective towards the child.

Air Kisses are used as greetings. The mouth does not make contact with the cheek

Hand Kisses are rarely seen now in the West but they were once a common greeting.

Saying goodbye

Just as greetings are made into a ritual, so are goodbyes. We signal a separation by first signalling our intention to end the interaction and finally by gesturing farewell. We do not usually part abruptly, as we want to assure the other person of our continued interest in them and that we want to see them in future.

A hug, handshake or kiss may accompany the goodbye, just as it does with the hello. Again, it will depend on the formality of the context and relationship. Sometimes, when people are saying goodbye to each other, they will part, turn and look back and wave.

The Vertical Wave uses the full arm with the palm facing out.

Common goodbyes

A wave is a common way to gesture goodbye. There are three main types of wave, and these are used in both greetings and farewells.

► **Sideways Wave:** In this wave, the arm is held up, with the palm facing forwards, and the hand is moved from side to side. In North America the whole arm tends to be used in a semaphore-type gesture.
► **Vertical Wave:** The arm is held up, with the palm facing the other person, and moved up and down in a patting gesture. This type of wave is used in France.
► **Hidden-Palm Wave:** The palm is kept facing the waver, who moves his hand back and forth towards himself. Although this looks like a beckoning gesture, it is a common wave in Italy.

If you no longer want to be part of a conversation at a party, you must first reduce the signals that indicate you are interested in the other person's conversation, for example, the number of supportive nods and agreement sounds you make, and how often you make eye contact .

▷ Shift your weight and place your hands on the arm of the chair.
  Or, if you are standing, point your feet away from the conversation.
▷ Move away from the other person slightly. Take a step back. If they
  don't get the hint, repeat this action.
▷ A sign that someone wants to escape from you is when they stroke
  the back of their hair or pull their jumper over their bottom. They are
  anticipating showing you the back of their body as they walk away.

**Sideways Wave:
the palm faces
forwards and the
hand is moved from
side to side.**

WANT TO KNOW MORE?

▷ Greeting
  **See chapter 12
  Getting on at work**
▷ Common gestures
  See Introduction
▷ Hands
  **See chapter 3
  Hands, arms and legs**

7 Getting on well

When you get on well with someone, your body will signal that you like that person, and it will also show interest, agreement and rapport. This chapter looks at how we show another person that we feel positive about them.

7 Getting on well
First acquaintance

Suppose you see someone for the first time in a social context. What do you do? Generally, we spend the first few minutes of our encounter checking the other person out and sizing them up.

If you are talking to the person, you may be concentrating on what they are saying, but you are also taking in a lot of information about them and forming a first impression that will last a long time and govern how friendly you are to them in future.

Assessment

When you assess someone for the first time, you check out their sex. Are they the same as you or different? You also see if you can work out how old they are. Are they older or younger than you? How attractive are they? Is this potentially a sexual or a platonic encounter? What is their status compared to yours? Do you need to treat them with added respect or deference? Finally, how similar to or different from you are they? How do their words, body language and voice give you clues as to their race, culture, class, education, occupation and nationality?

All of these factors influence how you behave towards another person, how comfortable you are with them and, therefore, how positive and open your body language is towards them.

Body language

You use body language to assess the other person through smiling and positive facial expressions. When you meet somebody for the first time, and when you meet them again, it is a convention to show pleasure.

Gestures and varying degrees of direct eye contact will encourage small talk, as you work out what you really feel.

When you first meet someone, you are likely to put on a positive
face as you work out how positive or negative you really feel.

Being positive

Open body language is our way of showing another person we like them and feel relaxed with them. There are specific gestures and movements that you can observe in others to see just how positive they are feeling about you. What if you like the look of them? Regardless of your sex or theirs, you will encourage them to get to know you by signalling interest in them and what they have to say.

WATCH OUT

If a person nods while you are talking to them, this signals agreement. But if they start to nod more frequently and more rapidly, it may mean they want you to speed up so they can interrupt.

Posture

Position: It has already been seen that people point with their feet to where they really want to go when they are talking to another person – perhaps towards an exit or towards someone else in particular.

The angle someone stands at also has significance. Generally, people do not stand face to face when talking in a social conversation. In fact, most people stand with their bodies at a right angle facing outwards towards a point halfway between both of them. This makes a triangle, with the third point of the triangle an open space, so that other people can enter the conversation if they want to. Your posture is likely to be inclined forwards towards the other person. You may stand closer to the other person or by their side. Your hand may touch an arm or a shoulder to encourage or show appreciation.

People who are attracted to each other, on the other hand, close off any point of entry by facing each other directly, preventing other people from coming into their conversation.

If a person is not welcome in a conversation, the two people talking to each other may allow them to come as far as standing at the third point of the triangle. However, they will not turn their whole bodies to welcome them into the conversation but instead look at them only occasionally. At the point they are willing to let more people into the conversation, they will open up their bodies and welcome them in. If several people want to join in, they are likely to stand in a circle talking to each other.

Eye contact: When you are interested in someone, you look at them and they look at you. Smiling is then used to show interest and agreement. It encourages the other person to talk or to continue a conversation. Raising and flashing the eyebrows quickly is another sign of positive interest that may happen at the same time.

Interest shows in the size of the pupils of the eyes. When you are interested in another person, your pupils will get larger. This is a totally unconscious gesture and impossible to control.

When you are very interested in something, or someone, you will also blink more. Again, this is not done consciously, so it is not something a person can fake.

Head position: At the beginning of the conversation, when you are slightly interested in the other person, your body is turned towards them and your head will be held up.

If your interest increases, you will cock your head to one side. Agreement is signalled by nodding the head up and down. If you nod once, it signals 'yes'. Nodding occasionally during a conversation is used to show that you are listening to the other person and that you are willing to continue listening to them.

Gestures: Gestures are open and encouraging. Showing your open palms towards the other person is intended to be both positive and encouraging.

Tilting the head at a slight angle shows that you are interested in the person you are talking to.

Holding the hand lightly next to the cheek is another sign of interest in the other person.

WATCH OUT

Body pointing
Your feet and body give away whom you are interested in. If you are standing in a group, your body will turn towards the person who most interests you. If you are sitting, your feet or knees will point towards them.

Making friends

We are all most attracted to people who are similar to us. Your friends are likely to share your values and attitudes, as well as many of your core behaviours. Researchers have discovered that we enjoy relationships with people most if they also have similar communication skills to us.

Rapport

Watch two people who are relaxed with each other and getting on well, and you will notice that they mimic each other's nonverbal behaviour. Their body movements match, and they speak at a similar speed and volume. If one person makes a particular gesture, the other follows. If one has their arms or legs crossed, the other will, too.

Having a rapport with another person means that we start to feel like them. Then we adjust our behaviour to be like them. We unconsciously go into rhythm with them, and our bodies are directly aligned.

Watch people sitting at a bar and notice how often they are in rapport.

This is known as **postural mimicry**, or matching and mirroring. Matching and mirroring are basically the same, but with one small difference.

With matching, you match the other person exactly. One person has their right leg crossed over their left leg; the other person has the same. One has their left arm resting on a chair arm, so does the other person.

With mirroring, two people adopt a mirror image. One has their right leg crossed; the other faces that person with their left leg crossed at the same angle.

Natural rapport body language

Matching and mirroring does not mean that all gestures and body movements are the same, but a significant number are. Observe two or more people who are naturally in rapport with each other. Watch to see if they match some or all of these movements and gestures:

- ▶ **Posture:** The angle of their backs and spine will be erect or bent.
- ▶ **Angle of the head:** It may be straight or tilted.
- ▶ **Arm and leg positions:** They may be open or folded.
- ▶ **Gestures:** These may be close to the body or away from the body.
- ▶ **Facial expressions:** Are they smiling, grimacing or angry?
- ▶ **Blinking:** Is it frequent or infrequent?
- ▶ **Speed and location of breathing?** Is it fast or slow? Is it from the chest or stomach?
- ▶ **Colour change:** The skin on the face and neck changes colour slightly with mood. A person's colour can be high, with a flush or blush, or pale. A colour shift in the same time in both people is an indicator of rapport.

The position of the legs and arms match, showing how in tune these two people are.

The voice

Rapport also causes people to adjust their voices to match another's. Have you ever noticed yourself picking up words or phrases from somebody you really like or admire? You may even change your accent unconsciously to fit in with a group of people. This happens to a degree as soon as you begin to build a rapport.

Listen for the tone and qualities of a voice. Does it sound low and deep, or high pitched or squeaky? Is there a particular accent? How about the smoothness or melody in the voice? Are the words rhythmic or clipped?

Notice key words and expressions, too. Are there any words that each person marks out with extra emotion in their voice? People often use signature words that have a special significance for them or are particularly used within their culture or place in society.

Deliberately building a rapport

If you are not getting on well with another person, you can make it happen. Build a rapport consciously by altering your body and voice to match some of their movements until you reach the point where it happens automatically.

Start by sitting at a slight angle to the other person, not directly facing them. If you are facing them and copy their body language, it will not be subtle enough. They may think you are mocking them through mimicry.

Take a snapshot in your brain of what they look like right now. Check the natural rapport body language list (see page 107), and notice all the areas where body language can change. This is the baseline you can work from. You can read the unconscious changes in the other person to see if you are producing an alteration in their feelings towards you.

Begin to match or mirror their body language, then notice what happens to their baseline. Look for subtle changes that signal rapport. For example, observe the colour of their skin. Does it change from light to dark? Or shiny to nonshiny? Or vice versa? How about the size of the lower lip? Is it getting smaller or bigger?

Notice also that the eye focus may change and the pupils will become bigger or smaller. The muscles in the face may become symmetrical or asymmetrical. Finally, the tone, pitch or speed of the voice may change.

As you align your body language to match the key movements and voice of the other person and you establish a rapport, they will start to feel at ease with you and see you as being like them. Your communication with each other will be enhanced and your relationship will grow.

As soon as you meet somebody and notice how they behave before and after they feel comfortable with you, it is easy to detect any changes of mood. This is particularly useful in business or selling when you need to be very alert to your clients' needs.

Young lovers hold hands as an ownership gesture.

Being in charge

If you look at a group of people who are getting on well, they all seem to be doing the same thing at the same time. In fact, there is always one person who is the unconscious leader. When that person changes position, or speeds up their speech, everybody else does, too.

If you need to establish a rapport with a group of people quickly, for example, if you are presenting a speech to an audience, observe who is leading the group. Make sure you match them. It is the quickest way for all the people to feel comfortable with you.

A good place to practise this is in a queue where people have been waiting quietly for a while. Notice who is matching whom and what happens when one of them shifts position. Practise identifying the leader and matching them. Notice if you can begin to lead the crowd.

Physical appearance

Physical appearance has a big influence on how you react to people. If you meet someone for the first time, you may be suspicious of them. But if the stranger dresses like people you already know, you are more likely to feel positive and open towards them immediately.

Changing your dress to fit in is a nonverbal way in which you can meet somebody on their home ground. We look for people like ourselves. They are the kind of people we feel most comfortable being around. We change our dress accordingly for interviews, for eating out, for a wedding or for going to a football match.

Changing clothes to look like other people signals a desire to adopt the conventions of the particular group. It means that, as soon as we arrive, they are likely to be pleased to make our acquaintance rather than feel threatened.

Football supporters emphasize they belong to one group by wearing the same clothes.

WANT TO KNOW MORE?

▷ **Personal space**
See chapter 5
Territory and personal space
▷ **Attraction**
See chapter 8
Attraction
▷ **Lack of rapport**
See chapter 9
Negativity

8 Attraction and dating

How do you use body language to attract a partner? Men and women are attracted to each other because of what they look like, but also because of the way they flirt and use their bodies to try to seduce and attract the opposite sex. It may surprise you to know how much of this is instinctive. You may have been using many flirtatious gestures without realizing it.

Basic attraction

What attracts you to a potential mate is to some extent an animal attraction. We all instinctively search for a healthy partner with whom to have children, whether we know it or not. We look for clues to confirm that the other person is male or female, and for clues about the state of our future mate's health and fitness.

The ideal woman

According to studies, men across the world are basically attracted to women who are youthful and fertile, with a clear skin and a shapely, hour-glass figure. They look for what makes women different from men, such as large breasts, longer legs, a narrow waist, full hips, thin eyebrows, as well as less facial hair. When women want to attract a man, they need to emphasize or fake the sexual characteristics that show they are women, and young and fertile. So they might wear high heels to lengthen legs, and an under-wired bra to make breasts look firmer.

The ideal man

Women tend to like men with small, pert bottoms, strong shoulders, eyes that are set far apart, thicker eyebrows than a woman's and hair on the chest. They view the lines on a man's face as attractive. A square jaw, strong cheekbones and a medium-sized nose are also seen as manly. A triangular-shaped torso is a sign of youth and vigour. When men want to attract a woman, they tend to pay more attention to their personal grooming.

The ideal man has a symmetrical face.

Both sexes

Some characteristics are liked in both sexes. Both men and women seem to prefer an oval, symmetrical face, high cheekbones, large eyes with long eyelashes, a short distance between the chin and mouth, and a medium-sized mouth.

Times change

However, being born with the perfect face and body won't necessarily bring you success in the dating game. For a start, fashion and culture mean our tastes can change, so that we choose a mate based on different criteria. For example, in the West, we now hold healthy, fit women to be more attractive than plumper women who were seen as the ideal a few centuries ago. Cosmetics and clothes can also change the way we look.

Most important, you can be more attractive than the average person but be unsuccessful in attracting a sexual partner if your body language makes you look disinterested. On the other hand, if you are fat and thin-lipped but skilled at displaying availability signals, you're likely to be highly successful in winning the love game.

Dating

When we want to attract a partner, we change the way we behave. If we are available, we show it. Women especially dress up, do their hair, wear jewellery and put on perfume. We all use our bodies, our gestures and face and eye movements to show sexual interest. How effectively we do this determines how successful we will be in attracting a partner. Some signals appear to be unconscious and are probably inborn. Some grooming and preening gestures are deliberately chosen.

Women move their bodies to show off their femininity. They use small gestures, close to their bodies, and animated facial expressions. Men try to appear more male by using dominant and controlled gestures, as well as sexual displays, such as pulling at their clothing around the crotch area.

Both sexes

Both men and women adopt an erect posture, pulling in sagging stomachs and sticking out the chest to look more youthful and toned. Other changes can also take place with attraction: pupil dilation, heightened muscle tone, rapid eye blinking and facial flushing.

must know

Love at first sight
When we look directly into the eyes of someone with an attractive face, it triggers the pleasure centres of the brain, producing feelings of love.

Showing availability

When you see someone unattached walk into a party, bar or club, the first thing you will notice them do is check out who else is in the room. Their body is saying, 'Here I am', 'Notice me, I'm a male/female' and 'I will not harm you if you come near me'.

Showing you're available

According to psychologist Peter Collett, people do this by looking fully around the room, first by moving just the eyes and then by turning the head to see who else is present.

Next they move into the room and walk around to check out potential partners at close quarters, rather like a salesman in search of prospects or potential clients. What they are doing is announcing very early on that they are available. By walking around, any prospective partners are far more likely to notice them than if they stay in a corner and do not move.

Once they have spotted a potential partner, they will, later on, circle around that person or move their position in relation to them, showing that they have narrowed their focus to one particular 'prospect'. The person they are targeting is likely to respond in kind if they are interested.

Different environments

In a competitive or noisy party or club environment, people need to make very open signal displays to win attention. They may choose to wear particularly revealing clothes, talk loudly, fool around or dance erotically or provocatively. All these make an obvious display of intention and make you stand out in a crowded space where more subtle displays might be lost because of the number of people. The advantage of animated movements is that they can be spotted at a distance by a prospect at the far end of the room.

In a quieter, less busy environment, an office for example, you will still see availability signals, however they are likely to be less animated. Men might stretch out in their chair, stick out their chest and pull in their stomach or, in the case of a woman, she might perch on the edge of the desk to reveal a leg or thigh. Because there is less competition and the room is probably smaller, these signals will probably get the attention of any prospective mates.

Both sexes

Both men and women use gestures to try to attract the attention of a potential mate.

Preening gestures such as hair flicking can signal interest from a distance. They may be something as seemingly meaningless as picking imaginary fluff from your clothing or cleaning your glasses. The gestures draw attention to your body.

Self-touch is useful as well. When you caress your own body, you draw attention to it and say to the other person 'Wouldn't you like to be doing this?' Self-touch includes stroking your own arms or face or legs.

Pointing is another sign. If you are interested in another person, you may point your foot or knee towards them. It shows where your mind is focused, even if you are talking to someone else. Leaning towards another person shows you want to get closer to them and enter their personal space. Watch the body and the head tilt to see how interested someone is.

Finally, nodding generally is an indication that you are trying to show increased interest in someone. It can be platonic interest, but it may signal specifically that you want to be closer to them out of sexual interest.

must know

Being the centre of attention
Where you stand in the room makes a big difference to the impact you have on other people. Standing in the centre of the room and moving around a bit will attract the highest amount of interest from others. In a bar or club, stand by the corner of the bar. Don't sit at a table or stand near the wall – in these positions, you are unlikely to be approached.

Watch where a woman points with her foot to see whom she may be interested in.

Women

Women use a greater range of signals than men to signal their availability and their interest in a man. They are also better at picking up men's courtship signals.

The shoulder glance is an availability signal.

Signalling availability

In fact, once a man and a woman have established that they are available, it's almost always the woman who makes the first move to show she's willing to be approached, though this may be so subtle that the man may not realize he's not the one to make the first move. She does this through a combination of seductive gestures and by showing she's safe, that is, not going to bite his head off if he approaches her.

Men read these signals from women and generally approach only when they have picked up enough of them, even if they do not realize this is the case. This is because men are afraid of being rejected or embarrassed. When they see the right body signals, they know their chance of winning a partner is high and try their luck.

Female signals

Women use signals to play up their femininity, making themselves look smaller and drawing attention to the softest parts of the body, such as the cleavage, neck, wrists and genitals.

Eyes

▶ **Eye contact:** If you are a woman who wants to attract a man, look across and catch the man's eye, then quickly glance away or down. This is usually repeated a few times to underline the message. You may also hold eye contact for slightly longer than normal to make sure that he notices.

▶ **Eyelash:** An extension of this is the eyelash flirt. This is a tiny flickering movement, raising the eyelashes very slightly so that, for a fraction of a second, the man sees more of your eyes.

▶ **Doe-eyes:** With this look, you glance at the man slightly sideways or through lowered eyelashes to enhance the effect.
This is the Princess Diana glance: looking up with 'doe eyes', while keeping the head and chin down. Men find this highly appealing, as the message is 'I'm interested', but there is also a child-like shyness to it.

With doe-eyes, the woman holds a man's gaze while keeping the head and chin down.

▶ **Shoulder glance:** Another form of this is the sideways glance over the shoulder. It looks quite shy but, in fact, is a forceful gesture. The shoulder is an erogenous zone.
The roundness of the shoulders mimics and reminds men unconsciously of the buttocks and breasts. A glance over the shoulder gives a man a quick sexual invitation and tells him to approach.

▶ **Smiling:** One of the most approachable things a woman can do is to smile. It makes her look safe and welcoming.

must know

Female space
A woman who wants to be approached should stand with her feet close together and pointing slightly inwards. This reduces the space she takes up and, by using gestures that are close to the body, makes her appear feminine and less dominant. Using too much space is a sign of power and authority, and may look masculine.

Red lipstick or slightly parted, moistened lips are used to attract a man

Head

▶ **Hair flick:** Whether a woman has long or short hair, she can use it to add to her come-hither messages. She flicks or tosses her hair away from her face or runs her fingers through it. This probably evolved as a gesture to show off youthful locks since, as we know from shampoo advertisements, bouncy well-conditioned hair is considered a sign of youth and attractiveness.

▶ **Licking and pouting:** Pouting and parting the lips slightly are other ways to give an invitation to a man to approach. Women's lips are generally bigger than men's, so showing them off draws attention to the fact that she is female. In addition, the mouth mimics the female genital area. When a woman is sexually aroused, the lips and genitals fill with blood and become darker and larger. Licking the lips mimics this sexual arousal.

Red lipstick has the same effect, reminding a man of the red genital area, which is why colouring of the lips has been used for thousands of years.

Body

▶ **Marilyn Monroe walk:** Rolling your hips when you walk shows off a feminine shape and draws attention to the genital area.

▶ **Sitting or standing with the legs apart:** Highlights the genital area.

▶ **Shoe fondle:** Letting your shoe slip half off your foot and playing with your feet in the shoe mimics the action of thrusting in sex.

Sitting cross-legged, a woman fondles her shoe with her foot.

- **Stroking the thigh:** Many women cross and uncross their legs, and caress their thighs to show how they want to be touched by the man, while drawing attention to the genital area.

- **Leg-twines:** Sitting with one leg entwined around the other pushes the thighs together and makes the leg muscles look more toned, which is a sign of sexual arousal. The toes may make small circles as an additional sign of attraction.

Crossing one leg tightly over the other draws attention to the woman's muscle tone.

The foot of the crossed leg points towards the man that the woman is interested in.

Men

Men may not have as much flexibility in their repertoire of attraction gestures as women, but they make the most of them to look macho and dominant, using up more space and open gestures.

In the cowboy stance, the man's fingers point down towards the genital area.

Male courtship/preening gestures

▶ **Crotch yank:** Pulling at the clothing around the crotch is an open reminder of manliness. Interestingly, one of the main users of this signal is Michael Jackson, who has used it increasingly as his face has become more delicately featured.

▶ **Cowboy stance:** Standing with the legs apart and the hands on the hips or thumbs in the belt displays the crotch. Again, this is a macho display.

▶ **Erect posture:** Standing with the stomach pulled in and the chest pushed out makes a man look younger, fitter and more manly, as it gives the upper body more of a triangular shape.

▶ **Tie straightening:** This is a specifically male preening gesture, which may be accompanied by grooming of the shirt sleeves and collar.

An erect posture makes a man look more virile.

Straightening the tie is a male preening gesture.

- **Smoothing the hair**: This preening gesture is the male version of a hair flick.

- **Legs:** These may be stretched out to occupy more space and create the impression that the man is bigger than he is.

Standing with the hands on the hips enhances a man's height and size.

► **Territory:** Men set up territories for themselves in a party situation. They take over a space and scatter their possessions around. Unlike women, they tend to stay in a fixed space but signal their presence by talking or laughing loud enough for the women to hear. Women tend to walk around more to show off.

A leg straddle is an attraction gesture.

Getting closer

Once the signals indicating that the woman is available have been given, and the man has decided he is interested, it is usually the man who makes the first approach.

WATCH OUT

Blushing and blinking
Facial flushing is a signal of sexual attraction during courtship for men and women. When a man is attracted to a woman, rapid eye blinking may take place.

In a nightclub or party environment, the man often approaches the woman from the side or behind. He may keep his chest thrust out as he walks towards her, sway, or thrust his pelvis forwards slightly.

The signals that follow are not learned behaviour but appear to be universal and unconscious.

Body

When the man approaches the woman, he moves into her personal space and she does the same to him, until one person gives a signal that the other has moved close enough.

When both people are interested in each other, they stand square-on, facing each other, aligning their bodies and blocking other people from entering the space between the two of them. This signal is visible to others, even if they are standing at a distance, so it is very effective in making sure other love rivals or people who might interrupt the conversation stay away.

Eyes

After their mutual attraction has become clear, both the man and the woman spend a lot of time looking into each other's eyes. The pupils will become large, and the eyes may be slightly moist. Each person will hold the other's gaze at length, and the woman may use doe-eyed looks, with the head slightly down in a flirtatious manner. The man or woman directs their look at the other person's eyes, lips, cheeks and eyebrows. Women seldom look away from the man's face during this stage of courtship, but men scan the area around them in the early stages of courtship, as if they are checking for potential rivals.

Touch

The first touch in a relationship is likely to seem accidental. In fact, it is a distinctive courtship gesture. The man may touch an arm or another non-sexual part of the woman's body. If she accepts the touch rather than pulls away, it is a sign that he can progress the relationship. This first touch is more likely to come from the man than the woman.

Before the touch, the couple may signal their interest in touching by laying their hands across the table so they are close to each other or reaching out with their hands.

Touch increases as the intimacy of the relationship increases. Touching progresses from a first touch to petting and caressing. The part of the face that encompasses the ears, nose and lips is often touched during a relationship because it is one of the areas that sends strong pleasure signals to the brain.

Playful gestures

Before kissing enters the relationship, the woman may continue to draw attention to her mouth by biting her lips or touching her chin and face. The woman often laughs and smiles at the man's jokes, too.

The woman may also play with objects. She may caress the stem or rim of a wine glass or her keys. Each may play with, or stroke, objects belonging to the other person.

WATCH OUT

Wrist turning
It's instinctive, but if one person's interested in the other, at some point they are likely to show off their palms and the inside of their wrists. This says: 'Trust me. I'm showing you my vulnerable spot.'

WATCH OUT

Lack of interest
The path of love isn't always smooth. Watch out for signals that indicate that interest is waning.
▷ A foot pointing away from you or towards a door is a signal that the other person may want to leave the conversation.
▷ Frowning, sneering or crossing the arms may signal defensiveness or hostility.
▷ Rolling the lips so they become thinner is also a negative signal.

Long-term relationships

In long-term relationships, love signals can often be seen even when neither person is speaking. If the relationship is strong, you will see the couple matching each other: standing or sitting in the same way or picking up on each other's gestures.

Because they feel bonded to each other, the couple stand close together but they give out fewer of the other love signals, as they have already negotiated the terms of their relationship.

Relationships in trouble

If the relationship has difficulties, you will spot the same signals of lack of interest as shown early on in a relationship.

For example, you may notice signs such as negative facial expressions, or gestures such as a foot pointing away from the other person (showing where they want to go). Notice also general signs of breaking of rapport such as a lack of matching in limb positions.

However, apart from general negative signs, it is difficult to spot infidelity from any particular

Couples in love nuzzle and snuggle like a mother and baby.

individual body language signal. Instead, it is important to recognize a person's normal behaviour and then look for changes in clusters of signals away from that baseline behaviour.

Happy relationships

One way to notice a couple in love is by the way they use baby and parent gestures with each other. When you are in love with someone, you act almost as if you are their baby. You may nuzzle them, kiss, hug or snuggle up to them. These are the same actions a mother makes towards her child.

WANT TO KNOW MORE?

▷ Foot pointing
   See chapter 4
   Body and touch
▷ Body mimicry
   See chapter 7
   Getting on well
▷ Disinterest
   See chapter 9
   Negativity

9 Negativity: boredom, discomfort and stress

Sometimes it all goes wrong. You feel negative, critical, bored, disinterested or threatened. You may express this negativity openly, for example by shaking your head. Or, where open expression is not an option, you may consciously try to mask your feelings. However, your body will still leak out your true emotions through tiny, involuntary movements and changes.

Deliberate gestures

There are some signals that we use openly to express negativity, knowing that the other person will understand immediately what we mean. There are cultural variations, but the following three are common in Western culture.

Head shake

The most common open signal for 'no' is the head shake. The head is turned from side to side, evenly from left to right.

It is thought that this signal has developed out of the action of a baby pushing away the nipple after drinking milk. The head shake is a universal signal, although in Ethiopia it is slightly different with the head moving to one side only then back to a neutral position.

In Greece and some parts of the Mediterranean, the head is tossed backwards and then moved to a neutral position instead as a 'no' signal.

A head shake is the common signal for 'no'.

The thumbs-down signal means that something isn't good.

Thumbs down

Pointing the thumb down with the fingers placed towards the palm and using a jabbing motion means 'It is not good' or 'bad news'. This is said to derive from the actions of the Roman emperors who turned their thumbs down to indicate that a gladiator could kill the person he had defeated in a contest.

Fist shake

When the negative feeling escalates into open hostility and aggression, an individual may shake his fist by punching out in front of him, or he may bang his fist on a table or punch into his own fist.

Fist shaking is a sign of aggression.

Boredom

You can't always show openly that you are feeling negative about a situation. It is important if you are talking to someone, or presenting in a business environment, to be aware of what other people are feeling and when they may be losing interest. Even when the other person is trying to look interested, check their body language: there will be leakage if they are feeling at all bored.

If you have lost interest in what another person is saying, you may well fidget, rest your chin on your hands, lean back in the chair or turn away to one side.

Although it is not deliberate, it will be obvious to other people you are bored. Boredom signals build up as the person's boredom gets worse.

The speaker should start to worry if they notice you checking your watch, arranging all your pens in a row, sharpening a pencil or pointing with your foot towards an exit.

They should worry even more when you close your eyes and slump even further forward onto your hands.

It might be time for a drastic change in subject or a cup of tea.

A fist supporting the head is a sign of boredom.

Boredom signals

Distraction is an obvious sign of lost interest. You scan or look away, turn your head away from the other person or find distracting things to do, such as drawing pictures in your notebook. You may keep your face towards the other person if you have to, but with a mouth-only, one-sided smile and a straying gaze.

Tiredness may follow. If no relief from a tedious situation is in sight, you will start to feel tired, your body will sag and you are likely to start yawning. Not all yawns mean that a person is bored, but they are a strong signal of boredom in conjunction with other gestures.

Look out also for repeated gestures. When you are bored or impatient, you tend to make the same action again and again, for example, wringing or clenching your hands, drumming your fingers, twiddling your thumbs, running your fingers through your hair or tapping your feet. As the boredom grows, so may the amount of movement.

Repeated gestures such as thumb twiddling indicate boredom.

The face is a giveaway, too. The bored person tends to keep a blank expression or a fake smile on the face. The jaw is clenched, there is tension in the face and a sigh may be let our inadvertently. The pupils of the eyes contract indicating that there is no interest.

Suddenly the head seems to need the support of a hand under it. Although this movement is similar to the expression of interest, when the hand rests on the side of the cheek, with boredom the head is completely propped up by the hand.

Finally, the whole body sags and slouches when you are losing interest. When you are really bored, the trunk straightens out and you will probably stretch your legs out straight in front of you.

Hair twirling is another sign of boredom.

9 Negativity: boredom, discomfort and stress
Disapproval and displeasure

Displeasure and disagreement may be shown openly or be masked. They range from slight signs that the other person is critical or disapproving, to open insult and conflict.

Disapproval

In most social situations, people will try to mask any feelings of negativity initially so that open conflict does not arise. The most common masks are consciously adopting a false smile or a straight face. A less conscious way to hide your emotions from the other person is to turn away from them slightly, or to cover your face with your hand, or to use a prop such as a cigarette or a piece of paper.

How do you tell when another person is feeling not just bored but negative about you? Here are some common signs:

Body: Watch for a closed posture. If you are in disagreement with the person who is talking to you, you are likely to sit upright and close off your body by putting barriers in front of yourself by folding your arms and crossing your legs.

Look out also for different types of limb barrier gestures. Some barriers may be partially disguised; some will be open. The range of such barriers that can occur are arm and leg barriers, disguised arm barriers, arm crosses, disguised arm crosses, leg locks, leg crosses and ankle and foot locks.

Head: Generally watch for more tension in the jaw, pursed lips and a tense face. Lowering the head, with the forehead pointing forwards and towards the floor, or glancing sideways, signals dislike of something or someone.

Rubbing an eye or pulling down an eyelid is a sign of discontent. Wrinkling the nose is a signal of disapproval.

The listener twitches the nose to one side as if moving away from a nasty smell.

Other gestures: The repeated tapping of objects or drumming of the fingers should be watched out for. If these become more intense, the feeling of negativity is growing.

Watch out, too, for fluff picking. A critical listener may pick imaginary bits of fluff off his clothing in an unconscious grooming gesture.

must know

Barriers
When we fold our arms or cross our legs or ankles, we are putting up a barrier to the other person. This is a signal that we feel negative about them in some way. Researchers have found that getting students to sit with an open posture and uncrossed arms and legs makes them more willing to learn and to hear what the teacher has to say.

The listener is feeling negative. She has her hand under her chin with the index finger pointing upwards and thumb supporting the chin.

Aggression and hostility

If we do not pick up on other people's negative feelings soon enough, they may deteriorate and result in conflict and aggression. As soon as this happens, openly attacking gestures will be used by one or both sides. It is clearly important to spot the signs of changing body language early on.

Two men size each other up with hands on hips.

Aggressive body language

The first place to observe this is posture. Aggressive body language is normally open. The body may be turned away at first. As hostility grows, the person makes their body bigger by standing tall and erect. They thrust the chest out, and place the legs wide apart. The head may also be thrust forwards, with the chin jutting out.

Putting the hands on the hips is another aggressive posture that shows off the crotch area. By exposing the most vulnerable part of the body, the person is showing that they know they can win a fight. Watch two people squaring up to each other.

Hostility may be accompanied by staring and a direct, aggressive gaze. A person may squint and narrow their eyes. Or they may frown, tighten and purse their mouth or snarl.

A deliberate sexual insult gesture.

Sexual insults

Many gestures are used deliberately in an aggressive situation to insult the other person. In Western cultures, these are often sexual in nature and suggest, to put it nicely, that the other person goes away and has sex.

Examples of these gestures are moving the arm upwards in a thrusting gesture, tilting the chin up, sticking one or two fingers up to the other person, butting the head or wagging the fingers.

Any other gestures that are used will tend to be larger and use more space to signal aggression.

Anxiety

When someone is feeling anxious, they use clusters of gestures that betray their nervousness. Watch the face and body for the giveaway signs that betray anxious feelings.

The fig-leaf pose covering the genital area is a defensive or anxious gesture.

Animals and humans behave in a similar way when they are nervous. They engage in activities that are not immediately related to their primary activity. These are known as displacement activities, or adaptors (see Chapter 1). Their function seems to be to get rid of some of the nervous energy that is building up because of the internal emotion and conflict being experienced.

People may play with objects such as cigarettes, keys, sleeves or rings; fiddle with or wring their hands; tap or drum their fingers or tap their feet. They often touch their head, too, by stroking their chin, touching their hair, face or ears, or rubbing their neck. Finally, they may chew their nails or hair.

These activities are often accompanied by a partial covering of the mouth, eyes or face with the hands when speaking, as if to put up a barrier

> **WATCH OUT**
>
> **Skin**
> The skin tone of a person who is anxious may change and become flushed or pale.

over these areas. Generally, a person's voice will betray their feelings, as they may clear their throat and be very hesitant when speaking.

Posture is a giveaway, too. An anxious person may look down at their shoes and shift their weight back and forth. Their body movements are likely to be jerky. Their arms may be high and folded, or they may cover their genital area with their hands and stand in a fig-leaf pose.

Cradles

A universal gesture of self-comfort that reveals the person is feeling very emotional is the head cradle. Footballers often cradle their heads in their hands when they miss a goal. The hands are put on top of the head, as if it needs to be protected. In fact, it is a substitute for a hug from a parent.

Of course, it is not always possible to make such a visible gesture. A more subtle form of cradle can be seen in general situations when the hands are put behind the neck to support it, as a form of self-comfort.

The head cradle reveals a need for self-comfort.

Defensiveness

A person who feels threatened or under attack shows how they are feeling in defensive body movements. These are tense, tight closed body movements that protect the body.

Picking fluff off clothing is a sign of defensiveness.

A person who feels threatened or under attack shows what they are feeling in defensive body movements.

The first thing to observe is size. While the person who is aggressive becomes larger, the person who is defensive becomes smaller to compensate. We do this instinctively because an aggressor is less likely to attack someone who doesn't seem a threat. A person of equal size will look more of a threat than someone who is small. Therefore the defensive person is likely to keep their head and chin down to cover their neck and bring their limbs close to the body to reduce their overall size.

Other movements will reinforce the message that they are not a threat to the other person. They may protect their genital area with a leg, hand or arm used as a barrier. The chest and face are also delicate areas, so barriers may be used here as well.

Generally, as with any negative emotion, the body language will close up. A reduction in size is likely to go along with smaller movements, as any large, expansive or quick movements might be taken as a threat or an attack. To stop sudden movement, the muscles in the body automatically become tense and rigid when the person starts to become defensive.

Watch out for this type of body language when you are talking to someone. If you begin to notice clusters of defensive signals in the other person, you should check whether you are using aggressive body language without realizing it.

We often do not notice when we are behaving dominantly, but try to notice what effect your behaviour has on your relationship with the other person. If you change your body language to become less dominant, they will change theirs and you will both unconsciously establish a rapport.

Watch out for closed body language such as arm and leg barriers.

WANT TO KNOW MORE?

▷ **Arm and leg barriers**
See chapter 3
Hands, arms and legs
▷ **Rapport**
See chapter 7
Getting on well
▷ **Defensiveness and anxiety**
See chapter 11
Power

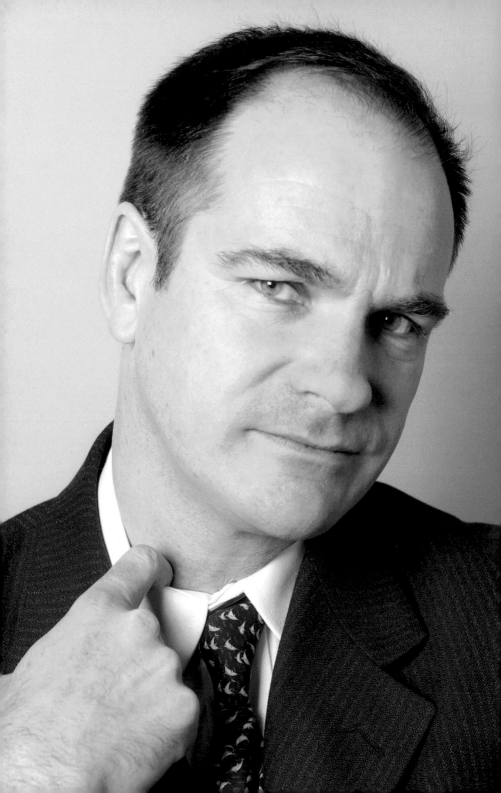

10 Lying, deceit and insincerity

No one can really keep secret how they are truly feeling. You can pay attention to every word you say, only for your voice and body to betray the words through facial expressions, gestures and twitches. If you are feeling at all negative about the lie you are telling, the emotions will creep out into micro-changes of nuance and mood in the body. This chapter gives you practical advice on how to detect these changes.

Lying

A lie is something that creates a false impression. Lying is something everyone does. It has been proved that it is part of our everyday lives – we lie in one-third of our interactions with others each day. That should make us experts at detecting lies, but it is easier to lie to someone else than know when you have been lied to. Lying is complex but, as ever, the body tells the truth, even if words are seeking to spin a different surface story.

People lie in all sorts of situations – on average once or twice a day. Lies can vary from quick lies such as 'How are you?', 'I'm fine, thank you', to emotion-laden lies that are hiding a crime.

Why people lie

The first reason people lie is because they want to make someone feel good about themselves, for example 'that outfit really does suit you'. These are white lies and occur frequently in everyday interactions.

At other times, you may lie because you are afraid of the consequences of telling the truth. For example, a child will lie because he knows he will be told off or punished by his parents for breaking a toy. To avoid an argument or conflict of some kind, someone who is late for work will say that their car broke down. Or perhaps you have done something wrong or illegal and you are afraid of being caught.

Lies also occur when a person wants to appear as a different person from what they really are, for example, if they don't feel successful or interesting enough, and are afraid they will be rejected if they reveal the truth. These lies may grow in complexity if a person tries to weave relationships around a new identity.

Look for clusters of gestures to indicate deceit, such as a finger covering (guarding) the mouth.

Another form of mouth guard is holding the hands in front of the mouth.

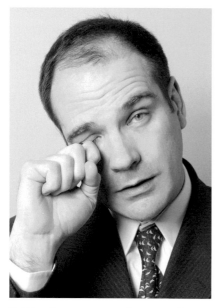

Rubbing the eye can mean that you are lying or that you sense the other person is lying.

Touching the nose, a signal of lying, may occur once or several times during a conversation.

Relationships

In relationships, people lie to present themselves to their best advantage to the other person. It may be a subtle lie – putting your most flattering photograph on an internet dating site, or exaggerating your achievements to win the attention of an attractive potential partner. The number one lie in relationships is the classic 'I will call you'.

In one study of university students, it was discovered that, in over three-quarters of couples participating, at least one of the people had lied about a past relationship. Generally, they lied for about one-third of the time to the person they were currently in the relationship with.

There's good news, though. As soon as people get married, they lie less to each other – only one-tenth of the time, according to one study.

How to spot a lie

In a study by Charles Bond of Texas Christian University, which was carried out in 60 different countries around the world, people were asked how they could tell whether someone was lying to them. In all the countries, the most popular answer was the same: 'If someone is lying to you, they look away.'

But this is not actually true. The signs of lying are much more individual and subtle, which is why it is so difficult to spot the poker player with the winning hand, even though 90 per cent of lies are accompanied by giveaway signals in the body and voice. Laboratory studies show that even when people are concentrating on trying to detect lies, they are only just over 50 per cent accurate – which is not much better than might happen by chance.

must know

A high amount of deception takes place between young people and their parents. University students consistently lie to their mothers – on average in 50 per cent of the conversations they have together.

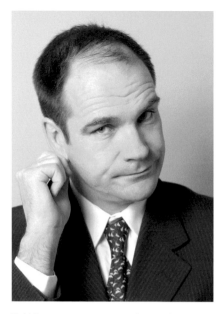

Rubbing your ear may mean that you have heard enough of someone's lies.

Scratching your neck means that you are not sure that you agree.

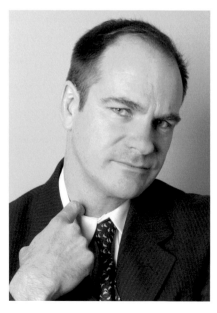

Pulling your collar indicates that you feel uncomfortable about something.

Putting a pen in your mouth shows that you may be under pressure.

Why are we so bad at spotting lies?

Gut instinct: We rely on our gut instinct too much. In fact, studies show that if you rely on your intuition to spot who is lying to you, you will be less successful than if you look for evidence of changes in gestures, micro-expressions and language.

Poor observation: We look for one gesture, rather than checking for clusters of gestures, which give a better indication of someone's emotional state. If someone keeps looking away, their hands are sweating and their breathing quickens, that may mean they are frightened or stressed but not that they are necessarily lying. This is why lie detectors are not always accurate – they can check for the physical signs of arousal but not actually prove that someone is lying.

Trust: We go through life expecting people to tell us the truth. We want to believe people and so we don't see the lies, even when we have spotted incongruent behaviour. It is as if we have a filter that cuts out the possibility of being deceived.

Con artists take advantage of this. They know that if their story is plausible and probable, we will give them the benefit of the doubt. Likewise, stage illusionists and mentalists know what we expect to see and use this to manipulate what we do see. Consistent liars find out what we are looking for in terms of deception and change their lies to ones that we won't detect.

However, we are adaptable. Professions that need to be more suspicious, such as the police and customs, seem to adapt their threshold of trust to become automatically more distrustful of others. The downside is that they can be too suspicious.

Lie giveaways

When people are not telling the truth, they tend to blink less, their voices can be tenser, and they move their hands and arms less. They do not generally give themselves away by using large gestures, and they are actually less hesitant in their verbal language than people telling the truth. It seems they are more guarded in their movements than truth-tellers and more rehearsed in their words probably because they are overconscious that other people could be alerted to possible incongruencies.

How to spot a liar

If you want to spot a liar, judge them first against the baseline of how they normally behave. Ask them a couple of questions about something that they have no reason to lie about and observe their body language. For example, 'What's the weather like outside?'

Then ask them the questions you suspect that they may answer by lying. Observe if there are any inconsistencies or changes in their body language between the first set of questions and the second.

Look for small changes. Watch out for the angle at which their head is held, in which direction their eyes move, how they are breathing, and whether they are showing any signs of tension such as sweaty palms or blushing.

As every person has very individual ways of lying, spotting the inconsistencies is the surest way of catching the deception. A truthful person is consistent and congruent in what they say and how they behave.

---

must know

A smuggler who has lied his way successfully through customs may give himself away at the last moment. Because the body may be unnaturally stiff when we are lying, as soon as we think we have got away with something, we relax, getting rid of tension but showing that we had something to be worried about in the first place.

Eyes

If you ask someone a question and they avert their gaze and turn away when answering, is that a sign of a lie? Ask the average person and they will say yes. Thus the term 'shifty eyes' comes from the common mistake made about liars, that is, that they won't look you in the eye.

The following are eye clues that show that some kind of internal conflict is going on:

▶ **Gaze:** Some liars do avert their eyes. Others have more eye contact than normal. They stare into your eyes to overcompensate and stress their honesty, as they know people expect liars not to be able to look them in the face.

▶ **Blinking:** Look for rapid blinking. When we are aroused or thinking a lot, we blink more – up to 100 blinks a minute, compared to 20 blinks a minute normally.

▶ **Beady eyes:** The pupils may constrict when we are lying.

▶ **Eye patterns:** Check the direction of the eyes. Do they move up and to their left to access a memory, or up and to their right to construct a visual image? Or maybe they move down to access an emotion? (See Chapter 2.)

▶ **Eye blocks:** The eyelids stay closed for a fraction of a second longer than normal during the answer, as if blocking the listener.

▶ **Eye twitches:** May happen involuntarily.

▶ **Eye touches.** Self-touch shows nervousness and discomfort.

Fidgeting and touching

When people are nervous, they fidget and touch themselves. This does not mean that they are necessarily lying but that it is an indication that there is some change in their emotional state, which is causing body language leakage. This could mean that they feel defensive or guilty, but you need to check other aspects of their behaviour as well.

Look for general fidgeting such as toe twitching, finger drumming, licking of the lips, neck scratching, pulling the

Some liars make more eye contact than normal. They stare into your eyes to stress their honesty, as they know people expect liars not to be able to look them in the face.

collar, gulping, head tilting, tense or restricted hand and arm movements, playing with the hair, tugging the ear and rubbing the eyebrows.

The body may be unnaturally stiff and the weight shifted onto the heels. The person may continually change position or shuffle their feet. Watch out for barriers such as crossed arms and legs, or using an object like a chair as a barrier.

Check for involuntary changes such as blushing and sweaty palms.

Masks

The simplest way liars try to cover up lies is by masking their emotions. They either keep a blank, expressionless face or they smile. As we have already seen, fake smiles are different from natural, spontaneous smiles. They are asymmetrical, they use the mouth but don't involve the eyes.

Micro-expressions

The part of our brain that processes emotions, the limbic system, causes an immediate physical reaction when we feel a negative emotion such as fear, jealousy, anger, guilt or shame.

However, we do not always want to show our emotions. So when we want to cover up our emotional reaction to something, the thinking part of our brain chooses to show a facial expression that will be more appropriate. However, that is not enough. If the emotion is strong enough, we can't hide it entirely. The raw emotion will betray our true feelings by leaking for a second onto the face. This is called a micro-expression.

A micro-expression can last for less than a second. That is so short a time that you may not even realize you have experienced or seen the emotion. It is possible to know this has

The shrug may be a conscious effort to deceive.

happened by videoing someone and slowing down the replay. Even though the fear or anger may pass across a feature of the face for such a short time, you will still be able to see the change.

Shrugs

Liars sometimes use shrugs to attempt to deceive. A shrug may be either a partial shoulder shrug or a hand shrug. With a hand shrug, the liar turns his palms upwards in a submissive, pleading gesture. It is as if the speaker wants our compassion.

Mouth covers

An unconscious gesture to look out for is the mouth cover. The speaker either partially or completely covers his mouth, as if he does not want us to see the lie coming out of his mouth. The mouth cover may be a tiny gesture. In its smallest form, it may consist of just the smallest touch to the side of the mouth.

The Pinocchio nose

Pinocchio's nose grew every time he told a lie. There is some evidence that when we lie, blood fills the nose, causing a tiny Pinocchio effect. To relieve the itchy feeling that accompanies this, we rub the nose. So the nose rub may indicate a lie.

More importantly, rubbing the nose acts as a mouth-cover substitute. This is because it is a self-touch gesture. The liar reaches to his face and touches his nose to gain some of the comfort that he would have by touching his mouth.

Whatever the reason, the nose rub seems to be a good indication of a lie. This is especially true if it is part of a cluster of gestures such as broken eye contact and hand barriers.

A famous example of this is Bill Clinton who, when questioned about whether he had had sex with Monica Lewinsky, touched his nose often as he said that he had not had relations with her. Touching his nose repeatedly could have meant a number of things but, combined with his other body language – stiff hand movements, tense body, increased sweating – and very carefully chosen speech, it appeared to indicate that he was lying.

Deceitful words

It is not possible to divorce the body language of a liar from his words. When you are not telling the truth, you have to think about a story rather than recall something that has happened, so your body language is going to give you away. Here are the many tell-tale signs that may accompany incongruent and inconsistent body language and provide further suspicion of deceit.

Verbal content

People tend to 'go around the houses' in their explanations about a subject when they are lying, according to Oxford University's Peter Collett. It is almost as if by not getting to the point any suspicions they may have will be removed. They may try to distract you by changing the subject.

But, liars avoid detail. When you listen closely, you will notice they are telling a long story but missing out many of the extraneous details about what people were feeling, what things looked like, and other irrelevant details that truthful people use to flesh out the feeling of the story. If you ask them to elaborate on their story, they may not be able to but will have to go back and repeat the story in the same way they originally told it to you. Someone who is telling the truth can spontaneously remember forgotten and irrelevant details, and often backtracks to add them. Liars have to remember the original sequence of the story they gave so that it remains consistent and they don't get caught out.

Defensive

Liars are likely to give short answers and may be defensive if pushed for more detail. They may answer your question by questioning you back, repeating what they said before or accusing you of not believing them. A common ploy is to answer your question with a question. Liars are also more likely to use words designed to disarm the other person such as 'honestly', 'truthfully', 'clearly', 'trust me' or 'you won't believe this but...'.

Unusual words

The liar's sentences may sound unnaturally structured or restrained. They may choose unusual words or expressions not used often in normal conversation. For example, they may say 'cannot' instead of can't or use a lot of negatives. This happens because they are trying to avoid making speech errors.

Control

Liars may try to distance themselves unconsciously from the lie by avoiding personal words like 'I' and 'me', and using impersonal expressions such as 'one', everyone' or 'nobody'. If they are worried about being asked questions, they may talk a lot or fake emotion to put themselves in control of the flow of the conversation and prevent you interrupting and questioning them.

Listening for lies

You can tell a lot by simply listening to a speaker's voice.

Listen out for the pitch of the voice. It may sound unnaturally high, as emotion causes a rise in pitch.

Note also the speed of the voice. It may be slower than normal because what the liar is saying is memorized rather than natural. They are also trying to stop the truth leaking through. However, silences are not a good guide, as the amount of silence in a conversation varies between cultures.

Another sign is the number of interruptions and hesitations. Liars often mumble, stammer or stutter, and fill their speech with breaks like 'ums', 'ers' and throat clearing as they try to keep their story consistent.

Although subtle, these signals indicate that there may be more going on than initially thought, and give you a reason to watch the body language very closely.

WANT TO KNOW MORE?

▷ Eyes
  See chapter 2
  Eyes, face and head
▷ Smiling
  See chapter 2
  Eyes, face and head
▷ Relationships
  See chapter 8
  Attraction

11 Power, dominance and submission

What are the secrets of power? Do you carry authority in your presence and gestures, as well as in your words? Why do some people make you feel inferior? How does your boss show that he is in charge? This chapter looks at the signals of dominance and submission in our physical behaviour.

Power

We talk about people carrying an 'aura of power'. In fact, there are a number of aspects to the physical behaviour of such people that tell us that they are dominant.

must know

Where to sit
If you want to look powerful, always sit at the head of the table. It puts you in charge because of unconsciously understood rules about space and territory.

Relative power

Even in the animal kingdom, it is obvious who is in charge. In primates, there are strict hierarchies of power within a group – which ape gets the first and best choice of food or mate depends on its status. It is the same in human society. Even though the strict rules of rank, class and privilege have been eroded in modern times, we are all very aware of our power relationship to others, and we work out where we stand early on in an interaction by the signals we give out and pick up.

Common signals

Here are some of the common body-language signals people use to win and maintain power:

Posture: A powerful person has a strong, straight-backed but relaxed posture. It says 'I am in charge' but 'I don't feel threatened'. Such people do not fight to hold their authority. They look confident, energetic and youthful.

Relaxation: Authority aims to look effortless. Powerful people have relaxed shoulders. They lean back in their chairs and appear as if they wear their responsibilities lightly and are unthreatened by the prospect of attack. They may even yawn, which makes the person look relaxed but is actually derived from a primate's signal of baring their teeth to say 'I'm dangerous'. Consciously we pick up the relaxation signal; unconsciously we pick up the message of who's in charge.

Size: Big is better in the power stakes. Height and size are equated with power because we see important things as large in our minds.

If you are tall, you stand above other people, and this is often interpreted that you have authority above them, too. That is why, until the most recent American presidential election, it was the rule of thumb that the tallest candidate would always win because the voters would see him as the most powerful. Interestingly, when the UK public has been asked about the relative heights of politicians in the past, they have misjudged the heights of different politicians by a considerable amount. Those they perceived as powerful they made taller, and those less powerful they made shorter. In other words, you can literally 'loom larger' in the consciousness of your observer.

Space: A powerful person uses up the space around them to emphasize their territorial ownership. To increase the impression of size, they may put their hands on their hips. This also emphasizes the sharpness of their elbows and says, 'Don't come too near, these could hurt you.'

This man, leaning back in his chair with his feet on the desk, is showing that he owns the territory around him.

Women and size

Tall women are in a difficult position, according to research by psychologists. Because of their height, they are naturally seen as authoritative, but because of their gender and cultural associations of femininity with smallness and delicateness, they can appear threatening to their superiors.

Small men

Small men behave differently when tall men are present. It has been found that a group of short men will find it harder to agree on an issue when a taller person enters the group. This is interpreted as being because they feel threatened by his relative height and therefore his implied power.

How to look powerful

If you are not naturally tall and want to look powerful, create the impression of relative height to give yourself instant authority. Keep an erect posture – flex your knees, stand up straight with your ribcage up and head held high – to make yourself as tall as possible. If everyone else is sitting down, stand while you are talking to them.

Make sure you do not lower your head to someone of equal or lower status. This is a submissive gesture and will make you look shorter.

Straddles

Straddles are a way of making your presence known in a group. In a standing straddle, you stand with your legs straight and apart. This gives the body a stable foundation and tells your audience that you are prepared to 'stand your ground'. It is also a very masculine stance because a man in this position displays his crotch.

Making yourself as tall as you can creates an impression of power.

Seating styles that display the crotch show dominance.

In a seated straddle, the chair is turned with its back to the group and you sit with your legs apart across the chair, facing the back of the chair. It looks as if you have a barrier between you and your audience but, in fact, this position allows you to lean forwards and be relatively aggressive in your words because there is a physical barrier between you and them.

Nonsymmetrical sitting positions

These often show a desire to be dominant. One powerful way of sitting is to keep your legs apart and stretched out in front of you, allowing you to occupy more space in the room.

Another is to bend one leg across the other to rest an ankle on the opposite thigh. This is a phallic gesture that shows off the crotch and it therefore becomes a macho display of power. However, it is not a position generally used by women, as it can be interpreted by others as being sexually provocative.

Bending one leg across the other to rest an ankle on the opposite thigh is a phallic gesture that shows off the crotch, which is a macho display of power.

Power walking

A powerful walk is one of two things: either very strong and vigorous, or very relaxed. Both styles of the walk are used by powerful people to say 'I am in charge' and 'I own this territory', as they walk in a way that fills up the space around them. Powerful people often accentuate this effect by turning their elbows outwards to show weapon-like sharpness.

American presidents are classic examples of power walkers. George W Bush uses a powerful walk. He swaggers when he walks, and makes himself look bigger by swinging his arms, showing off their muscle tone by turning them outwards. This is different from a normal walk because it makes the palms face away and down.

George W Bush uses a power walk.

Touch

A powerful person walks ahead of other people. However, when leaving a room it is more powerful to go last and to usher others through. Since, as we have seen, touch is such a potent symbol, someone who wants to dominate can use the touch of an open palm on the back of another person to guide them, and show immediately that they have authority. Place your hand between the shoulder blades of the other person and press lightly to guide them. This mimics a parent–child relationship, with the person doing the guiding in the parental role.

Touch, generally, is such an invasion of our personal space that it is something we grant as a privilege only to those we know very well. We are so aware of the force of touch that we go to great lengths not to touch strangers, even in a crowded bus or train. Between two people of unequal status, the dominant one touches the inferior first. It will be taken very badly if the touch is initiated the other way around. Higher-status people also touch lower-status people more frequently, as if to emphasize their relative authority. Therefore, a doctor is more likely to touch a patient than the other way around, a teacher to touch a student, a boss his secretary and so on.

Touch and gender

Men touch women more than the other way around. In studies of couples walking together, men tend to keep women on their dominant side, that is on their right side if they are right-handed. What this means is open to interpretation, but it is suspected that there are still associations between gender and social inferiority. Researchers have found that when men touch women, it is often seen as a signal of power or sexual advance. When women touch men, it is seen as a gesture of intimacy.

Handshakes

A dominant handshake is one in which the palm of the powerful person faces down. To be powerful, extend your right arm decisively forwards, grasp the other person's hand so that their palm faces up, and pull them slightly into your space. At the same time, touch their wrist or elbow with your left hand. An extended arm is an assertive movement that cannot be ignored. Touching or gripping the other person's arm at the same time gives you control of the interaction. Touching the other person on the back when greeting them also works as a way of establishing who has the power and leadership.

A dominant handshake establishes the powerful person's advantage.

Speaking

Dominant speakers underline their speech by using expansive and emphatic gestures. They move their hands forwards and away from the body, just as a conductor beats out the rhythm of the music, to assert the power of their words.

The most powerful person in the room tends to speak the most and for the longest. They also interrupt other speakers more. But if you want to sound powerful, then speak more slowly and more deeply. Mrs Thatcher was trained to do this during the time she was prime minister because a lower-pitched voice is perceived as more powerful than a high or squeaky one. A deep voice is a sign of higher testosterone and therefore more physical power.

WATCH OUT

How much eye contact you make with another person will be what they remember most after meeting you. However, more than 5–7 seconds of direct gaze at any one time is seen as threatening rather than powerful.

Eyes

Powerful speakers are happy to look at other people. They use more general eye contact with their audience than submissive people, and look at everybody involved in the interaction. Dominant people look directly at others, rather than allowing the gaze to drift towards other parts of the face. Eye contact lets other people know who is in charge.

In our everyday interactions, we look less at others of equal status when we are speaking to them than when we are listening to them. However, powerful and higher-status people, or people who want to dominate, look at others more than average when they are speaking.

Narrowing the eyes is powerful, as is having narrow eyes. This is because of the visor effect that has been mentioned previously (see page 37). Lowering the eyebrows and narrowing the eyes makes a person look angry and confrontational, and therefore dominant.

Smiling

Dominant people use closed-mouth smiles. They keep their lips together when smiling, while extending the corners of the mouth to produce a thin, elongated smile. Keeping the mouth closed gives an impression of tightly kept secrets and determination. Studies have shown that the more testosterone a man has, the smaller his smile, which makes the smile appear more macho as well.

Dominant smiles are tight-lipped.

Politicians and power

Politicians have to create a consistent aura of authority and power while seeming accessible and not off-putting to voters. It is a complicated balance because they are constantly being watched by millions of people through the press. Not all of them carry it off easily, but those that do are successful because of their body language, rather than the actual content of their speeches. They use powerful signals and, at the same time, appeasing signals.

▷ **Show how nice you are:** Politicians smile a lot. Look for genuine smiles by the creases next to the eyes. Ronald Reagan was particularly good at real smiles.

▷ **Emphatic gestures:** Politicians like to underline powerfully the points they are making. Tony Blair uses a lot of emphatic hand movements.

▷ **Kissing babies:** Holding a baby diverts any aggression away from you. It signals that you are powerful but likeable.

▷ **An accessory wife:** A loving spouse holding your hand or hugging you shows what a lovable person you are. Cherie Blair often hugs Tony in public.

▷ **Applause:** Be photographed with lots of people applauding you. It make you look popular.

▷ **Be careful whom you stand next to:** Tony Blair adopts more dominant gestures than usual when he stands next to George W Bush, but the President is clearly the one with the upper power hand.

Submissive body language

Submissive people feel vulnerable, and their body language shows it. While dominant people use open body language, submissive people use closed, fearful and defensive language. They act to varying degrees as if they are under attack.

Size

If you are submissive, you keep your body small, hold your limbs in and make any gestures small and close to your body, using up little space. This closed stance makes you less conspicuous and also protects you from attack.

If you are tall but do not want to be intimidating, you can counteract the powerful message of your height by stooping when entering another person's space. You approach them and their world metaphorically submissive, as well as physically.

The head is often ducked, tilted or dipped in front of a more powerful person. This allows the eyes to be averted from the other person to show that no threat is being offered. Lowering your body is a sign of submission, which is why curtseying and bowing are overt signals used to acknowledge that someone has higher status than you. In addition, you can make your body smaller by stooping or sitting when the other person is standing.

Stance

There are several ways people stand and sit to show that they are letting other people dominate. They stand with straight, scissored or crossed legs so the legs are tightly pressed together. The stance

The submissive scissors stand.

may be asymmetrical, with the weight on one leg and the other bent behind, or just in front of, the straight leg.

An asymmetrical submissive stance.

Submissive people may sit with their legs pushed back into their own space so they do not come into anyone else's social space. The legs may be tightly crossed at the thigh or ankle.

These positions all conceal the crotch area and limit the amount of space the person takes up. It also allows the body to be in contact with itself – a form of self-touch.

Eyes

Interrupted eye contact: Not looking someone in the eye or interrupting eye contact is a sign of submission. To show that you are no threat to the other person, you will avert your eyes or flick your eyes to one side, then the other. The temporary removal of eye contact tells the other person you are not going to put up a challenge. At the same time, the dominant person is blocked from the submissive person's view for a fraction of a second, allowing them unconsciously to notice escape routes.

Eye opening: Another signal is the widening of the eyes. The weaker person makes their eyes look bigger by opening them wider for a fraction of a second so that they appear more innocent, babyish and unthreatening. This awakens an unconscious urge in the dominant person to protect the weaker person.

Raising the eyebrows is also a gesture that further signals a willingness to give up power.

Gestures

Submissive people may self-touch to reassure themselves when they feel threatened or under stress. It reminds them of the comforting touch of their mother when they were a baby.

They are also likely to show their palms to the dominant person as an unconscious pleading gesture. (This is the 'I'm no threat, please don't arrest me, officer' gesture that many people use when they are hoping to avoid arrest.) It confirms that they offer no harm to the other person.

Submissive people tend to be more still and muted in their movements than powerful people.

In this way, they signal that they do not intend to be aggressive towards the more dominant person. Animals freeze or curl up when under attack, and humans, too 'freeze up', when they feel they are in danger.

Showing the palms signals that the person is not a threat.

WANT TO KNOW MORE?

▷ Submissive and dominant palms
   See chapter 3
   Hands, arms and legs
▷ Standing
   See chapter 4
   Body and touch
▷ Stress
   See chapter 9
   Negativity

12 Getting on at work

This chapter looks at how to apply body language in the workplace. Who is trying to dominate? How can you present yourself effectively at a meeting or interview? Why is your client so resistant to buying? Reading the body language signs will make all the difference to your success at work.

Different professions

People skills are key in the workplace. How you communicate with the people around you, how you form relationships with them and how you motivate and influence them are vital to success in your career. These skills can only be fully realized if you have the ability to read and use body language in context.

Different professions need different body language skills. Teachers need to blend authority with warmth, openness and confidence to keep their students on track. The caring professions, such as nursing, ideally use open body language, with a lot of smiling, eye contact and touch to the shoulders to show reassurance and comfort. In the retail industry, shop assistants will sell more if they smile a lot and use direct eye contact, head nods and head cocks to encourage customers to express their needs.

For politicians to be effective they need to look powerful but at the same time electable. They use appeasement signals such as smiling and open hands to show they are approachable and down to earth.

Finally, people on TV work particularly hard to win our affection. They smile a great deal and use lots of eye contact with the audience, as well as deliberately flirtatious and exaggerated expressions and gestures. They want us to 'fall in love' with them.

Presentation

In all these professions, the clothes you wear emphasize the role and the effect you want to achieve, from the structured business suit to the overdone hair and makeup of the international star, designed so that we notice every movement of their head and change in their mood.

How you style your hair and wear your makeup, as well as the colour and formality or informality of your clothing, is so important that it can determine whether you are seen as being good or bad at your job.

Always dress appropriately for the job.

Meetings

Modern employment is full of meetings. To win over an audience or an important client, make sure that you look right and sound right, and that you have prepared your body language as well as your presentation.

When you are giving a presentation at a meeting, you will get a positive reaction if your body language is generally open and relaxed. If you have closed or nervous body language, it will provoke a negative or bored reaction. It is also important to be energetic when you are talking, though obviously not so energetic that you overwhelm any introverts in your audience.

Be conscious in every work situation to establish a rapport with the other people there. When in a group, get in touch with whoever appears to be the natural leader of the group and everyone else will follow.

A confident presenter has an open and relaxed stance.

An unconfident presenter will look tense and have a tight posture.

Seating plans for meetings

Make sure that you know the rules of personal space and territory. These rules also apply to where you sit at a meeting. With your choice of seat, you will unconsciously influence your relationships with colleagues and clients. The rules depend on the shape of the table.

Imagine that you are seated at a square table for a meeting. The person next to you on your right-hand side will be most attuned with what you have to say and tend to want to agree with you. The person who will feel least on your side will be whoever is sitting across from you at the table. This is because the table puts a physical barrier between you that acts as a mental barrier too.

Where you sit at a table may make the difference as to how others at a meeting perceive you.

If everyone seated at a round table is of equal status, they are likely to feel relaxed.

Round tables can work very well for meetings. People tend to feel more relaxed with each other, but only if everyone is more or less of the same level in the company. If someone is much more senior or junior, the rules for square tables apply.

If a long table is used for a meeting, do not sit with your back to the door. You are not going to have the same level of authority when you speak as you would do away from the door and at one end of the table, which automatically gives more importance to what you say. If there are only two of you, sit so you are both across the corner of the table. This allows easy eye contact, while the table acts as a slight division so you keep your personal space.

Getting on with your colleagues

Any group of people has its own dynamic that depends on unconscious power arrangements, rather than the given job titles and status within the pecking order of the organization. Body language will betray the subtle power struggles going on in a meeting of people in a business.

Who is the boss? The following clusters of movements are all expressions of dominance, ownership and territoriality. They let you know that your colleague thinks he is the boss.

He is relaxed, with his hands clasped behind his head and his feet up on the desk. He is leaning back in his chair against a wall or a desk, or he is straddling the chair, or has his leg draped over one of the chair arms.

Be careful. If you threaten him, he is likely to use dominant gestures to stay in control.

Who likes whom? Watch out for people who do not have a rapport with anyone else. They may not make eye contact and turn away from the group, and keep an unsmiling face.

In contrast, look for people who like their colleagues. They will smile a lot, look relaxed, face their body fully towards others and stand or sit in close proximity to the group.

WATCH OUT

Whenever you are speaking or presenting in any group situation, make sure that you are giving the right messages. Here are some key points to remember.

▷ Keep alert. Look at everyone and don't turn away from the group. Make sure you do not just talk towards one person.
▷ Give listening signals to whoever is talking: good eye contact and nodding the head.
▷ Avoid folded arms, hands on hips or slouching back in your chair.
▷ Avoid fidgeting, which suggests nervousness. Leave your hair, ears, pens and hands alone. No foot tapping or finger drumming.
▷ Speak clearly and not too quickly.

Selling

In selling you can use your general meeting skills while being aware of some specific applications. There is a sequence of steps to a sales process, starting with building a rapport with the customer and ending with them agreeing to buy.

In selling you can use your general meeting skills while being aware of some specific applications. There is a sequence of steps to a sales process.

▶ First of all, you need to establish a rapport with the customer. Quickly build a relationship with them so that they trust and like you. Win their approval. Be likable. Make plenty of eye contact, and match and mirror body language. Make sure you do this subtly, though, rather than mimic them.

▶ Secondly, question the other person and find out why they might want to buy your product from you. Look and listen: good sales people listen as much as they speak. Use interest signals to get the other person to open up about what they are truly looking for.

▶ Thirdly, influence the customer by proving to them that they want your product. Speak about your product confidently. Use animated, open body language and gestures. If there is more than one customer present, make sure you look at everyone.

▶ Look for body language that may indicate an objection, for example, a loss of rapport or sudden barrier gestures such as crossed arms that show discontent or boredom. Stop and ask for their reactions to what you have told them about your product so far. Make sure that you restore rapport.

▶ Finally, ask the customer to come to a decision to say 'yes'.

A relaxed presenter means that the customers are engaged and interested.

The closed body language displayed here means the customers are no longer in rapport.

Winning rapport

To make the sales process effective, you need some key body-reading skills. Look for signs of rapport. If the other people feel positive about you, you will see signs of body posture matching. By mimicking your body language, they are showing silent approval of what you are saying. You can test how much you are in rapport with the group by trying to lead them (see page 111). When you speak, shift your position – your arms, legs or angle of the back – and see if they follow suit.

If they do not follow you, who are they following? When one person shifts their position in the group, others are likely to follow if they have a rapport. There is always one person in every group who is an unconscious leader, and it is not always the person with the top job title. Make sure you gain rapport with that person by matching their body language (see pages 106–107).

Don't overplease

Some salespeople seem to think the way to win a sale is to toady to the customer. Yes, the customer is king, but be careful not to use low-status, pleading body language such as smiling or laughing too much, rubbing or washing your hands together, mimicking rather than mirroring the client's body language and bowing your head deferentially to the client too often.

Be careful also not to talk down to the client. You can look overconfident in a number of ways: by leaning over them and using their space; loosening your tie or putting your jacket on the back of the chair, unless they have suggested you do so; tilting your head back so you talk down to them; leaning back in your chair; or sitting with one leg crossed over the thigh of the other leg in a macho display.

Look for approval signs

Watch out for signs that the customer is happy to go along with what you are saying. A big signal is an open, genuine smile that uses the eyes as well as the mouth. They may also nod to encourage you to continue speaking.

Good eye contact shows they are interested, while head tilts show they are listening. Pursed lips show they are concentrating and, finally, open hands and palms mean they are friendly and receptive.

Look for negatives

Watch out for negative signs, too, and be alert to sudden changes from open to closed body language. Look for fake smiles and tightly crossed arms and legs as an indication that the client is suspicious or defensive.

If their nodding becomes more rapid, it may indicate they want to interrupt you. Standing with their hands in their pockets means they are suspicious. If they turn their eyes away from you, it may mean a lack of interest or dislike.

If they touch the back of their head, it indicates they want the conversation to end – it is as if they are placing their hand

WATCH OUT

Hand steeples are a good indicator that the buyer is feeling positive. However, if a hand steeple follows a series of negative gestures, such as arm and leg barriers or hand-to-face gestures, it means the buyer is feeling good about themselves but negative towards the salesperson.

in the direction they want to turn to – away from you. Finally, the feet or body pointed towards an exit means that they want to be somewhere else and that your sales pitch is failing.

Evaluation and making decisions

There are significant clusters of gestures and body movements that indicate a client is thinking about what you are saying and coming to a decision.

Their body will be relaxed and open, and they may lean forwards, showing interest, with the chin resting on a hand, a direct gaze and pursed lips.

Watch their hands, too. They may be steepled, either pointing upwards or downwards. This means the buyer feels confident. Or they may stroke their chin or the lower part of their face, as if they are ruminating while stroking an imaginary beard.

These gestures mean that they are either in the process of judging how your sales pitch fits with their way of thinking or that they are close to a decision.

By stroking his chin, this man signals that he is evaluating what is being said.

Sales seating

Be very aware of space and territory when selling. Sit in someone's favourite chair and you have already alienated your potential buyer before you have even started.

For a sales meeting, ideally choose to sit with your customer to your right. They have a safety barrier of the corner of the desk between them and you but you are still at an ideal angle to keep lots of side-on eye contact.

If you are forced to sit opposite your customer, find an excuse to move your chair slightly so that you can sit diagonally across from them. Push some papers across the table at an angle and inch your chair around so you show them what is on the papers.

If the meeting involves several clients and sales people, avoid having all the people from your company sitting on one side of the table with all your clients lined up opposite, like two tribes going to war. If possible, use a mixed seating arrangement: salesperson, client, salesperson, client.

Interviews

An interview is, in effect, a sales meeting in which you are selling the product – 'you' – to a purchaser – 'the interviewer'. Creating the right kind of chemistry with the interviewer through body language could clinch the interview for you.

In an interview, the recruiter will generally see more than one candidate with similar qualifications, knowledge and skills. 'Chemistry' or 'fit' between the interviewee and interviewer can be the winning factor. You can learn to create chemistry by being aware of your body language.

Making your entrance

As soon as you are seen walking through the door, you are making an impression, so make sure it is the right one. Slowing down or dipping your head as you enter will look anxious and tentative. Rushing in can also seem nervous. Keeping an erect posture with your head held high in contrast looks confident.

Pause at the door, smile at the interviewer and walk through decisively. You are aiming to appear personable and warm, as well as business-like.

Transfer any coat, briefcase or handbag into your left hand to leave your right hand free ready to shake hands confidently with the interviewer.

Handshakes

Be aware of your handshake. Avoid bonecrusher or limp/dead-fish handshakes (see pages 92–95). If you have a tendency to sweat or have cold hands, make sure you have wiped your hands or warmed

must know

Dealing with nerves
It is obvious when interviewees are nervous. They fidget and self-touch, they break eye contact and look down at the floor. If you are genuinely nervous, remember you can change your emotional state by changing your posture. If you adopt a confident posture, you will feel more confident inside as well. How you feel influences how you behave. But how you behave can also influence how you feel.

This interviewee dips her head and looks overanxious as she enters the interview room.

them up before you enter the room. Use a firm handshake. Hold out your hand horizontally so that your palm meets the other person's at the same angle.

Remember that a handshake can give you a lot of information about someone. Notice how the interviewer offers their hand. When they clasp it, do they turn your hand so that their palm is facing down, putting themselves in the dominant position? Do you both walk towards each other into each other's personal space equally or do they pull you towards them? Do they release your hand first and push it away? Are they relaxed or nervous? Is their hand warm, cold, dry or damp? Is their arm fully extended or relaxed? Do they touch you with their other hand?

This interviewee is fiddling, which makes her look nervous.

Eye contact

Make eye contact with your interviewer(s) when listening. If there is more than one interviewer, make sure you make equal eye contact with both. Remember that too much eye contact can seem aggressive, so scan the upper triangle of the face (from the eyes to the forehead), rather than stare directly into the other person's eyes without interruption. Break your eye contact when you are thinking of an answer. It looks natural.

Sitting

Keep your posture confident and relaxed. A good trick is to take a deep breath when you sit down and lower your shoulders. It will make the interviewer respond positively to you. Make sure you do not slump down in your chair or lean back away from the interviewer. It will look as if you are not interested. Instead, sit back into the chair so that you are well supported and, if you can, rest your elbows on the chair arms.

Personal space

Be aware of rules on personal space. Make sure your chair is positioned so that you can chat easily without invading the interviewer's territory. If you break the unwritten space rules, you could scupper your chances of success.

This woman looks relaxed and is making a good impression.

Open body language

Avoid leg and arm barriers and closed body language – you will just look defensive or submissive. Keep your gestures open and relaxed.

If there is a desk between you and the interviewer, sit back slightly so you have room to move freely. If you want to emphasize a point, keep your palms open and towards the interviewer to look friendly.

At the same time, be aware of how relaxed or formal the interviewer is. Stay in tune with them and let them set the tone for the interview. If you relax too much and are far more laid-back than they are, you will appear either sloppy or overconfident. If, on the other hand, you are too formal, they will find it hard to relate to you.

Matching

Get into rapport with the interviewer as quickly as possible. If you are not mimicking each other's body positions naturally, do it consciously. Match the angle of their back and position in the chair. Notice how they are breathing. If they talk quickly, they are probably breathing high in the chest. If they talk slowly, they are probably taking deep breaths. Get into their rhythm for a few minutes. After a while this will become automatic.

Watch while you speak

Be aware not only of your own body language but also the body language of the interviewer. Let their body language signals be your guide as to the level of their interest. Are they

---

must know

Cultural differences in business
▷ People in Italy have smaller personal zones than they do in Germany, and more touching takes place during business dealings.
▷ In Spain and Italy, body movements are more animated than those in Germany, where they are more contained. There are also more interruptions and talking over other people than in Germany.
▷ In China, nodding and eye lowering are used to show listening. Interrupting is not acceptable.

bored? Interested? Defensive? In agreement? Disagreement? When you make a point or give an answer, how do they respond? Notice if their body language suddenly changes. Interviewees frequently speak for too long, so be aware if the interviewer starts to nod more rapidly or tap their fingers. They may want to interrupt you.

Show interest

Vary your facial expressions to show enthusiasm and interest. When they speak, lean forwards, nod, or rest your forefinger to your chin to show your full attention. Lower your eyebrows, even frown slightly, to show concentration. Part your lips slightly. Also, make sure you avoid arm barriers when you are listening, as well as when you are speaking.

Be definite

Use your hands to emphasize points when you are speaking, but be careful not to use aggressive gestures such as making a fist or punching the air. Keep the conversation free of interruptions.

Leakage

Be aware of any possible leakage in your gestures when you are being interviewed. Prepare for the interview and rehearse answers to any difficult questions that you expect to be asked. This will allow you to feel relaxed during the interview, which will come across positively in your body language. Otherwise your body language could inadvertently make you appear deceitful or cause you to look as if you are avoiding an issue.

Saying goodbye

When you say goodbye, allow the interviewer to instigate a handshake. Return it with a firm handshake and then be aware that they will probably usher you from the room, as they are the dominant person in the situation. Finally, make sure you end the interview with a smile and eye contact.

WANT TO KNOW MORE?

▷ **Saying hello and goodbye**
   See chapter 6
   Meeting and greeting
▷ **Nervousness**
   See chapter 9
   Negativity
▷ **Open and closed body language**
   See Introduction

Need to know more?

Brief bibliography

Axtell, Roger E: *Gestures: The Do's and Taboos of Body Language around the World*, John Wiley & Sons, 1991

Bandler, Richard: *Magic in Action*, paperback, Meta Publications, 1984

Bandler, Richard and Grinder, John: *The Structure of Magic: A Book about Language and Therapy*, Science and Behaviour Books, 1976

Beattie, Geoffrey: *All Talk: Why It's Important to Watch Your Words and Everything Else You Say*, Weidenfeld and Nicolson, London, 1988

Beattie, Geoffrey: *Visible Thought: The New Psychology of Body Language*, Routledge, 2003

Birdwhistell, Ray: *An Introduction to Kinesics*, Louisville, University of Louisville, 1952

Collett, Peter: *Book of Tells*, London, Doubleday, 2003 http://www.thebookoftells.com

Collett, Peter: *Foreign Bodies: A Guide to European Mannerisms*, London, Simon and Schuster, 1993

Collett, Peter: *Social Rules and Social Behaviour*, Blackwell, Oxford, 1977

Darwin, Charles: *The Expression of the Emotions in Man and Animals* (3rd ed.), New York: Oxford University Press, (1872) 1998

Ekman, Paul: *Emotions Revealed: Understanding Faces and Feelings*, Phoenix, 2004

Ekman, Paul: *Telling Lies: Clues to Deceit in the Marketplace, Politics, and Marriage* (2nd ed.), New York, W.W. Norton & Company, 1992

Ekman, P & Rosenberg, E: *What the Face Reveals*, New York, Oxford University Press, 1997

Fast, Julius: *Body Language*, M Evans & Co Inc, 2002

Hall, E T: *The Hidden Dimension*, Doubleday and Co, New York, 1966

Hall, E T: *Silent Language*, Doubleday and Co, New York, 1959

Hartley, Mary: *Body Language at Work*, London, Sheldon Press, 2003

James, Judi: *Body Talk at Work: How to Use Effective Body Language to Boost Your Career*, London, Piatkus, 2002

James, Judi: *Sex Signals: Decode Them and Send Them*, London, Piatkus, 2004

Jaskolka, Anna: *How to Read and Use Body Language*, Foulsham, 2004

Lloyd-Elliott, Martin: *The Secrets of Sexual Body Language*, Ulysses Press, 2001

Mehrabian, A: *Nonverbal Betrayal of Feeling*. Journal of Experimental Research in Personality, 5, pages 64–73, 1971

Mehrabian, A: *Silent Messages*, Wadsworth, Belmont, California, 1971

Mogil J D: *I Know What You're Really Thinking: Reading Body Language like a Trial Lawyer*, 1st Books Library, 2003

Morris, Desmond: *The Human Zoo*, Cape, London, 1967

Morris, Desmond: *Intimate Behaviour*, Cape, London, 1971

Morris, Desmond: *Peoplewatching: The Desmond Morris Guide to Body Language*, London, Vintage, 2002

Pease, Allan: *Body Language. How to Read Others' Thoughts by Their Gestures*, Sheldon Press, 1997

Pease, Allan, Pease, Barbara: *The Definitive Book of Body Language: The Secret Meaning behind People's Gestures*, Orion, 2004

Quilliam Susan: *Body Language: Make the Most of Your Professional and Personal Life by Learning to Read and Use the Body's Secret Signals*, Carlton Books Limited, 2004

Russell, J & Fernandez-Dols, J M (Eds.): *The Psychology of Facial Expression*, New York: Cambridge University Press, 1997

Schelflen, A E: *How Behaviour Means*, Garden City, Anchor, 1975

Sommer, R: *Personal Space: The Behavioural Basis of Design*, Prentice Hall, Englewood Cliffs, New Jersey, 1969

Wolfe, C A: *Psychology of Gesture*, Methuen, London, 1948

Websites

- Articles on different aspects of body language including lying and attraction: www.selfgrowth.com
- Links to many academic and general websites on body language: www3.usal.es/_nonverbal/papers.html
- General interactive nonverbal site: http://nonverbal.ucsc.edu/
- Useful articles on body language: www.lifepositive.com/Mind/psychology/body-language/body-language.html
- The Mehrabian model: www.businessballs.com/mehrabiancommunications.html
- Body language at work: www.ivillage.co.uk/workcareer/survive/prodskills/articles/0,156472_176844,00.html
- Articles about Albert Mehrabian and communications: www.kaaj.com/psych
- Useful article on cultural difference: www.uclan.ac.uk/facs/class/languages/teib/unit5b.htm
- Useful resource on body language training: www.bodylanguagetraining.com/
- Introduction to the subject: www.findarticles.com/cf_dls/m1608/n7_v14/20946890/print.jhtml
- Body language and sales: www.smallbusinesssuccess.biz/free_articles_body_language.htm
- All aspects of nonverbal communication introduced: www.questia.com/PM.qst?a=o&d=28053073
- Article – NLP and rapport: www.inspiritive.com.au/bodylanguage_article.htm
- Useful site providing links to articles: www.cis.hut.fi/_parvi/Kie-98.505/body_links.html
- How people use body langauge: www.selectassesstrain.com/hint6.asp

Index

adaptors 19
affect displays 19
aggression 138
anger 20
anxiety 66, 140–141
arms 56–57
attraction 114–115
availability 116–125
    men 122–125
    women 118–121

bar chats 83
barriers 137
blushing 126
body 60–63
    availability 121, 126
body language
    aggressive 138
    at work 174–189
    closed 24
    open 24
    open at interviews
        188
    submissive 168
    types of 19
boredom 134–135

cigarettes 66
clusters 18
courting 68
cradles 141

dating 115
deceitful words
    156–157
defensiveness
    142–143
disapproval 136–137
disgust 22

emblems 19
emotions, reading 23
expressions 20–23
eye contact 34–35
    and interviews 186
    positive 105
eye movements
    36–37
eye patterns 38–39

eyebrows 36
eyes 32–39
    and lying 152
    and speaking 166
    availability 119,
        126–127
    blinking 126
    gazing 32
    pupils, 34
    submissive 170
    winking 28

face 40–41
facial expressions 40
fear 21
fingers 55
fist 133
friends, making
    106–111

gestures 19
    negative 132–133
    playful 127
    positive 105
    power 160–161
    submissive
        170–171
goodbyes
    at interviews 189
    saying 98–99
greetings 90–91

hand movements 49
hand positions
    52–55
hand steeples, and
    selling 182
hand to face gestures
    55
hands 48–55
    gestures 26–27
    palms 50–51
handshakes 92–95
    and interviews
        184–185
    dominant 165
happiness 20
head movements
    44–45

head positions 42–45
    positive 105
head
    availability 120
    nodding 42
    shaking 132
homes 81
hugging 96–97

interviews 184–189

kissing 97

legs 56–57
liar, spotting 150, 151
lies
    giveaways 151
    spotting 148–150
lifts 81
lying 146–155

meeting 102
    and greeting 88–97
meetings 176–179
micro-expressions
    154–155
mouth covers 155

nature versus nurture
    17
neuro-linguistic
    programming 38–39
nonverbal leakage 23
nose, Pinocchio 155

ownership gestures
    109

palms 50–51
parking spaces 73
personal space 74–83
    and interviews 187
    cultural differences
        84–85
    influences on 78–80
    invasion 76
    public space 82–83
physical appearance
    111

pointing 57
postural mimicry 107
posture 60–62
    positive 104
power 160–163
preening gestures
    122–125
presentation, at work
    174–5

rapport 106–109
    winning 181
regulators 19
relationships
    and lying 148
    long-term 128–129

sadness 22
seating plans
    177–178
    at home 81
    for sales 183
seating, public 83
selling, 180–183
sexual insults 139
shoulders, shrugging
    28, 155
sitting positions, and
    power 162–163
smiling 40–41, 167
speaking 166–167
stance, submissive
    168–169
status 63, 65
surprise 21

territory 72–73
thumbs 51, 133
tongue, sticking out
    28
touch 64–69, 164–165
    availability 127
touching rules 65
touching, and lying
    152–153
transparency 109

walking 63
    and power 163

Collins **need to know?**

Further titles in Collins' practical and accessible **Need to Know?** series:

Digital photography
All the kit, techniques and tips you need to take great photographs

192pp   £8.99
PB   0 00 718031 4

Golf
All the kit, techniques and inspiration to get into the game

192pp   £8.99
PB   0 00 718037 3

Zodiac types
Yourself, your friends and your family revealed

192pp   £7.99
PB   0 00 718038 1

Watercolour
All the kit, techniques and inspiration you need to get into painting

192pp   £8.99
PB   0 00 718032 2

Card games
All the rules and tips you need to start playing over 60 card games

192pp   £6.99
PB   0 00 719080 8

Yoga
All the tips and techniques you need to get healthy in mind and body

192pp   £8.99
PB   0 00 719091 3

Pilates
All the tips and techniques you need to get a lithe, flexible body

192pp   £8.99
PB   0 00 719063 8

Guitar
All the gear, techniques and tips you need to play the guitar

192pp   £9.99
PB   0 00 719088 3

DIY
All the know-how you need to get doing it yourself

192pp   £8.99
PB   0 00 719447 1

Weddings
All the facts, advice and inspiration you need for the perfect wedding

208pp   £9.99
PB   0 00 719703 9

Drawing & Sketching
All the techniques and inspiration you need to start drawing

192pp   £8.99
PB   0 00 719327 0

Birdwatching
All the tips and techniques you need to get into birdwatching

192pp   £8.99
PB   0 00 719527 3

The World
All the maps and facts you need to know in today's world

192pp   £7.99
PB   0 00 719831 0

Dog Training
All the ideas and techniques to transform your dog into a well-behaved, sociable companion

192pp   £9.99
PB   0 00 719980 5

Knots
All the tips and equipment you need to know how to tie knots

192pp   £9.99
PB   0 00 719979 1

Kama Sutra
All the ideas and techniques you need to enjoy a fantastic sex life

192pp   £9.99
PB   0 00 719582 6

To order any of these titles, please telephone **0870 787 1732**. For further information about all Collins books, visit our website: **www.collins.co.uk**